NOW IS THE
ACCEPTABLE TIME

A MODEST MEMOIR OF A MEMORABLE LIFE

Cover Photo: Hazel standing in front of the *Steam Power Plant* on the Asbury Park Boardwalk.

-1930's

NOW IS THE ACCEPTABLE TIME

A MODEST MEMOIR
OF A MEMORABLE LIFE

KELLY WALKER EDWARDS

Disclaimer

This is a memoir containing nonfiction content based on events and experiences shared with the author by the main character. Certain liberties were taken throughout the book for the sake of the narrative. Some names, places and identifying details have been altered or changed.

Copyright

Hazel Gordon Walker

DEDICATION

To Mommy
(GG)

My dearest friend and literary muse, who only saw the best
parts of me even when they were in pieces.

~

FORWARD

Dear Reader,

Every morning she combed my hair before school and prepared my favorite bowl of lump less cream of wheat with a pat of butter in the middle for breakfast. I was allowed to sip from her favorite coffee cup and sometimes she let me taste the remaining cake batter on the wooden spoon from the mixing bowl.

I was an inquisitive child, often too much into grown folks business, but always respectful because I knew better. Still, she allowed me to speak without interruption, share my opinions authentically, and patiently answered all of my nagging questions with sincerity.

Later in life, we were shopping buddies, reading enthusiasts, travel companions and confidants. My daily existence for many years was filled with her essence and frankness.

These experiences with my Grandmother enabled me to fiercely hold onto her stories and cultivate the memories we shared.

With homage *Now Is The Acceptable Time* to share them with you.

Thankfully,

Hazel's Granddaughter

Kelly

QUOTE

"IN THE END,

WE'LL ALL BECOME STORIES."

- MARGARET ATWOOD

CHAPTERS

1   LANCASTER VIRGINIA   Pg #12

2   HARLEM NEW YORK   Pg #31

3   ASBURY PARK NEW JERSEY   Pg #45

4   ACQUAINTANCE   Pg #58

5   CONNECTION   Pg #64

6   HOME   Pg #72

7   FAMILY   Pg #82

8   LIFE   Pg #100

9   TIME   Pg #114

10 CLOSURE   Pg #120

FOLKS

PAPA ALEC AND NORA
(GRANDPARENTS)

JULIA AND MAURICE
(PARENTS)

BABE
(JULIA'S HUSBAND)

LINA
(STEP-GRANDMOTHER)

ROSE AND RED
(AUNT AND UNCLE)

ELIZABETH (REESE), LOTTIE, AUDREY, CLARENCE, GEORGE, JAMES,
THOMAS, ROBERT, ANDREW, WILLIAM
(SIBLINGS)

DANIEL
(HUSBAND)

MARGARET/MAGGIE AND MORTON
(IN-LAWS)

ABENIA, MARGARET, ALEX, PRISCILLA, PHYLLIS, BILLY
(CHILDREN)

KELLY, KOREY, KOURTNEY
(GRAND AND GREAT- GRANDCHILDREN)

MARIE
(BEST FRIEND)

SONNY AND STACY
(SON-IN-LAW AND GRANDSON-IN-LAW)

ALFRED
(ROSE'S HUSBAND)

ADDIE, FANNIE, TOMMY, LAWRENCE
(AUNTS AND UNCLES)

NOW IS THE ACCEPTABLE TIME

~

CHAPTER 1
LANCASTER VIRGINIA

Located amongst vivid green shades of lush acres is Lancaster County, where wide oak trees are firmly planted along miles and miles of fields and crops. I have envisioned the birthplace of Hazel, my grandmother, for many years as a forbidden island where awful events occur, and people spend lifetimes hiding generations of indiscretions.

Lancaster is also remembered as a beautiful oasis filled with extra-large wooden two-story homes with wrap-around porches that hold wicker rocking chairs and tables with crocheted doilies. As a child, both descriptions of Lancaster existed for my grandmother who was born in the winter of 1911. Hazel's parents Julia and Maurice were twenty and unmarried when she arrived. Maurice left soon after her birth to serve in the military. He was a handsome man, small in stature with dark wavy hair and a shadow of a mustache. Julia was soft spoken with thick long chestnut hair full of waves that met curls on the end as you see in the ocean. Her eyes were almond shaped and kind. Both Julia and Maurice had fair complexions and could pass for a race different from the one they identified with. However, in the late 1800s growing up on the farms of Lancaster provided them with a sense of equality. They were removed from the many racial adversities occurring in other parts of Virginia and through-out other towns in the United States.

Julia moved to Maryland with the offer of work from a family member when Hazel was a toddler. She did not want to leave her daughter, but the emotional abuse she endured from her stepmother Lina was too much to endure.

Papa Alec married Lina a local woman from a prominent family in Lancaster. Lina lacked physical attractiveness and a nice demeanor. She was demanding, mean spirited and consumed with greed. Lina like the rest of the Garrison family was accustomed to having and getting what she wanted, and Lina wanted Papa Alec. He was a tall rugged man, with steel grey eyes, well-liked in the community, a productive farmer, barber, and oyster fisherman. He often allowed less fortunate neighbors the pick of his harvest and the ability to collect eggs from the chicken coop. Nora, his first wife, mother of his children and Hazel's loving grandmother was small and shapely with soft caramel skin and shoulder-length dark hair. Nora was rumored to have run off with some man leaving her children and distraught husband, but it was later revealed she was forcibly committed to a mental facility and remained confined there until her death. Similar to the women journalist Nellie Bly wrote about who were unwillingly placed in mental asylums by their husbands who didn't want them anymore. Sadly, it was evident Nora was incapable of standing up to Lina and her family to prevent her departure.

Unfortunately, Julia's plans of securing a job and creating a home to raise Hazel took longer than she anticipated. Hazel was five years old when Julia returned to the farm. Attempts to visit or correspond with Hazel were intercepted by Lina.

One day, Julia showed up joined by her husband Babe and their three small children, a girl Reese, and two boys George and Robert. Babe told Papa Alec and Lina he and Julia didn't have much, but it was only right that Hazel be raised with her siblings, so he and Julia were there to take Hazel back to Baltimore. Hazel was thrilled to see her mother and welcomed the kinship of her newfound siblings.

Hazel had a hard time containing herself and holding in the joy she felt, but she knew she better around Lina who was already displeased with the unexpected visit. Hazel and her siblings played under a tree within hearing distance from the front porch. She heard Papa Alec say, "It's okay if Hazel wants to go." Lina was quick to interject and say "This child is not going anywhere without you paying for all the years we have been raising her!" Lina threatened to contact the authorities if Babe and Julia didn't pay immediately. Lina's family had connections and Julia knew what Lina was capable of doing, look what happened to her mother, Nora, when she got in her way. Julia was afraid Babe would be arrested and what would happen to her and her other children.

Hazel's eyes soon puddled, and the tears trickled slowly down the same cheeks that were moments earlier widened with a smile and laughter. She said goodbye to her siblings not knowing when she would or ever see them again. Julia hugged her tight and softly whispered "I'm sorry" in her ear. Babe swiftly gathered Reese, Robert, and George and put them in the car. Reese didn't want to leave her sister and grabbed Hazel's hand. They had a fleeting moment of an alliance that sisters share accompanied by the fear that they may not see each other again.

The days and nights seem to melt into each other as Hazel grew up. She spent countless hours tending to her chores of laundry, cooking, and cleaning. Hazel found comfort with her animals on the farm, especially Trixie her beautiful horse. Trixie was her only friend since she wasn't allowed to have friends or visitors. She tried making friends with classmates as a student at Northern Neck Academy but was often teased and taunted for being light skinned. Also gathering with other young people after Sunday morning church service at Mountain Baptist was out of the question. Hazel had to stay close to Lina and leave immediately after church with her and Papa Alec in their Model T-Ford. On the ride home, Hazel was reminded to get out of her good clothes and get dinner started.

Lina always complained about having some ailment that prevented her from doing things around the house. As Hazel prepared the family dinner Lina spent her time entertaining relatives in the parlor, in particularly her younger brother. He came to the farm every Sunday dressed up in the same suit and tie, his hair greasy and slicked back and he smelled like burnt ashes mixed with soap. His laugh was thunderous and often startled Hazel in the nearby kitchen.

After dinner, Hazel would retreat to the barn with her friend

Trixie. She enjoyed the quiet time in the barn brushing Trixie's mane and dreaming about the endearing life her siblings were probably having in Baltimore. It was the only time she could be away from the house where Lina dominated, and Papa Alec complied. Lately, Lina's brother would find his way out to the barn after his second helping of food. He would begin idle talk about the weather and how he liked horses too. Hazel was uncomfortable with him being with her in the barn and would quickly finish brushing Trixie and return to the house to clean up the kitchen. She wasn't used to talking with people and felt if he was Lina's brother, he was most likely a lot like her.

The flowers were blooming on the farm and you could smell honeysuckle coming from the bushes surrounding the barn. Spring was a favorite time of year for Hazel. She thought it was a time of new beginnings the bursting out of all things that slept during the winter. Perhaps, she would also wake up to a new beginning, one in which she felt safe, nurtured and happy. Hopefully, that could be possible even after eighteen years.

It was another Sunday dinner of cooking, cleanup, and retreating to the barn. These days Hazel spent her quiet time alone reading books, she had collected from school or those donated by congregants at the church. Trixie was gone. Papa Alec had to shoot her after she was injured. It was a few years earlier on a rainy day before dawn. Trixie was frightened when he swatted a whip in her direction in an effort to train. Trixie rallied up and fell hard on a pitchfork near a haystack. Another reason for Hazel to harbor disdain for her grandfather, who she once adored as a young girl. It was difficult for Hazel to visualize Papa Alec as a protector anymore. His inability to censure Lina over the years for her approach and behavior in raising Hazel was cowardly. Lina's brother took full advantage of Papa Alec's lack of dominance on the farm and continued to prey on Hazel.

It was a long drive home from church this particular Sunday. The Model-T fluttered and stopped suddenly. Hazel had to crank the engine with the bar to get it going again. Lina wasn't able to help; she said her fingers were numb and she couldn't hold the crank bar. Lina always had an excuse to avoid anything that resembled work. But she could spend hours standing and trying on clothes in the dress shop in town. Papa Alec was in Chesapeake for a few days working on the Oyster boat. As much as Hazel was displeased with her grandfather, she still valued his presence on the farm. Lina was even more contumelious in his absence.

Today was Lina's brother's birthday and Hazel was instructed to bake a special cake for the occasion. She had already made a large breakfast of scrambled eggs, ham, and biscuits before church. The dinner she prepared was fried chicken, potatoes, cabbage, and cornbread. Everything was either picked or plucked fresh from the farm. Lina and her brother enjoyed the meal and birthday cake followed in the parlor. Hazel was exhausted and fell asleep in the barn while reading. She didn't hear Lina's brother enter the barn tonight nor did she feel his stares as she slept. His smell is what awoke her, but she was unable to speak or move. His hand covered her mouth and the weight of his body bound her. Hazel's eyes remained fixated on the horse saddle hanging from a high rapture. She forced her mind to focus on the methodical way she would prepare Trixie for her morning ride.

1. Brushing her mane a few times.

2. Placing the saddle on her back over the left side.

3. Securing the straps underneath her belly.

4. Straightening the saddle with a slight tug.

Over and over Hazel repeated and visualized these four steps in her mind. She never blinked as tears gathered and then gushed.

He had his way with Hazel that evening in the barn on his birthday. Her beloved barn, the only place on the farm where she felt secure surrounded by her books and fond memories of her time with her friend Trixie. But now the barn incased the forceful loss of her virginity along with the shattered fragments of her heart.

Days turned into weeks and weeks turned into months as Hazel struggled to move forward. Everything around her remained the same as if what happened in the barn did not occur. Consequently, missing several monthly menstruations was the affirmation of the incident. Hazel told Papa Alec what happened when he noticed her avoiding the barn and not being able to keep food down after she ate. It was easy to see her behavior was different and she was more recluse. Lina refused to believe Hazel and accused her of sneaking in the barn with a local boy. She then said it was probably Mr. Johnson, a married prominent businessman who she saw Hazel speaking with when they went into town recently.

Lina didn't know that when she saw Hazel talking with Mr. Johnson, she was asking him if she could ride into Richmond with him and his wife to see a doctor, she heard rumors about. Mr. Johnson and his wife took weekly trips into Richmond, a nearby town, so he could conduct business. Hazel knew it would be difficult to get away with Lina watching her every move, but Lina was planning a trip soon to see her sister and that's when she would travel with the Johnson's.

They arrived in Richmond mid-afternoon and Hazel agreed to meet back up with The Johnson's by 6 pm to return home to the farm in Lancaster. She found the small yellow house with green striped awnings on the corner facing a collection of large weeping willow trees. It was exactly as described from the town folks she overheard talking. The street was clean and quiet with manicured lawns and shaped hedges. Hazel thought maybe she could live on a street like this one day. She would welcome visitors and offer them extra helpings of desserts as they sat on her porch rocking and laughing.

The sound of a door slamming shook Hazel and she realized she had been standing in front of the yellow house for quite some time. She walked slowly up the steps and knocked on the front door. An older black woman answered with a look of disapproval. Although afraid, Hazel asked if the doctor was available and if she could see him. The woman stepped aside and pointed to a closed door at the end of a narrow hallway. Hazel walked gingerly trying not to make too much noise when her shoes hit the hardwood floor. She knew the woman was watching her and didn't want to look back. Finally, she arrived outside the door and waited for it to open.

Hazel hid the elixir underneath her undergarments and slips in her bedroom dresser drawer. She followed the directions given by the doctor in Richmond to drink two sips until the bottle was empty; one dose in the morning and one dose before bedtime. She spent all the money she saved from selling her books at the town auction on this concoction and hoped it would work. Seven days passed and the bottle was empty. Hazel's stomach had grown and there was no sign of her menstruating.

Each day Lina would tell Hazel she knew all about Mr. Johnson and how he did the same thing with other young girls in Lancaster. She threatened Hazel that Papa Alec would lose the farm if her family knew the truth. Lina convinced Hazel to tell everyone it was Mr. Johnson's baby, and this would enable Papa Alec to keep the farm. Hazel remained silent when anyone inquired about her condition. Lina did all the talking. She exaggerated about how Mr. Johnson took advantage of Hazel and how he was going to pay dearly for bringing this shame on the family. Nothing or no one could stop Lina when she wanted something. This time it was protecting her brother and getting

Mr. Johnson's money.

Lina had a history of being dishonest about so many things including when she pretended her shoulder was injured, mostly when work needed to be done around the farm that required lifting or when Papa Alec was out of town. Like the time when Papa Alec was away overnight on one of his oyster fishing jobs. Lina and Hazel were riding home from church in the Model-T Ford. The car stopped suddenly in the middle of the road. Before Hazel had the chance to wonder why they were stopped, Lina jumped out of the automobile, retrieved the crankshaft from the trunk, walked to the front of the Model-T, and lifted the hood slightly. While holding the hood up with one hand she proceeded to use the other and turn the crankshaft over and over clockwise until the engine started. There was no mention or evidence of an injured shoulder or any other body part on that hot afternoon.

The beautiful baby girl was born in December during a snowfall so deep that it covered the barn. Only the top peak of the roof was visible from Hazel's bedroom as she looked out the window. She was nineteen years old and now a mother.

The connection with Abenia was instant. She was a striking resemblance to Hazel; fair skinned, prominent nose, and smooth chestnut colored hair. Papa Alec kept saying how much Abenia also looked like Hazel's mother Julia. It was a long time since Hazel saw Julia and she ceased wondering when she would return. Julia was a grandmother now and didn't know and probably did not care.

Hazel spent the next year bonding with Abenia as Lina continued her quest to secure funds from Mr. Johnson. Hazel overheard her in the parlor speaking with some of her family members about filing a complaint with the authorities to force Mr. Johnson to pay for the care of Abenia. Hazel knew how harmful it was to accuse Mr. Johnson. He and his wife were well-respected residents in Lancaster and were always nice to her. But she remained silent. She was even more afraid of what could happen to Abenia if she disobeyed Lina. Maybe Lina's brother would show up and take Abenia, she imagined. Papa Alec instructed Lina's brother that he wasn't permitted on the farm anymore after she told him what had happened. Lina put up a fuss at first, but later agreed it was best not having her brother around to secure her plan. She did not want anyone to become suspicious.

Hazel prepared Sunday dinner; pork roast, corn on the cob, collards, and biscuits while Lina and Papa Alec were at church. She was not attending Sunday services since the birth of Abenia. The congregants said she was not allowed because she would be a negative influence on the other young ladies. Hazel was disheartened about this decision because she enjoyed church and wanted to share this part of her life with Abenia. She felt a sense of abandonment when she was shunned by the church and did not understand how Lina with her contemptible ways was considered an upstanding member.

On Monday, Hazel was ordered by Lina to wear one of her good dresses on Wednesday because they would be going into town to meet with Mr. Johnson's attorney. Hazel had hoped Lina's attempts of obtaining money from Mr. Johnson were over. She had accepted the way her life was on the farm. She also dreamed that when Abenia was older they could leave together and go to Baltimore to find her siblings or perhaps New York where her Aunt Rose and Uncle Red, Papa Alec's and Grandma Nora's children were now living. Rose and Red fled the farm when Hazel was younger and never came back. They had been tormented by Lina for years too.

Once in town, Lina escorted Hazel to the courthouse. They were seated in a room filled with faces of town people she recognized. Mr. and Mrs. Johnson were sitting in the front and they did not look at Hazel when she entered. Lina told Hazel that when they asked her about the baby's father, she was to tell them it was Mr. Johnson's. That would be the only way Papa Alec could keep the farm and she and Abenia could remain living there. Hazel was having a hard time breathing. When they called her to speak her legs wobbled so much, she thought she was going to fall. As she sat, she could see Lina mimicking words with her lips. She then looked over at Mr. Johnson and his wife who was sobbing. Hazel was asked to give her full name, her age and where she lived. She stated my name is "Hazel Gordon and I am nineteen years old. I live on the Gordon Farm in Lancaster County." She was then asked if she had a child, Hazel answered, "Yes, a daughter." She was asked, "Who is the father of your daughter?" Hazel did not answer. She was asked again, and she did not answer. Hazel was asked if the father of her child was in the courtroom, Hazel looked at Mr. Johnson and said loudly, "NO!"

She proceeded to tell how Lina told her to tell everyone Mr. Johnson was the father of her daughter to get money from him. "Lina and my Papa Alec know who my daughter's father is and they know it is not Mr. Johnson." Hazel could see the anger in Lina's face as she passed her when running out the courtroom.

She could not live with this lie any longer and felt relief stopping Lina's plan. She also knew her life would never be the same after defying her.

Hazel walked miles before finally reaching the farm. She couldn't remember how she managed to see her way back when her vision was distorted from tears and dust along the road. Abenia had been picked up by Lina and Papa Alec from the neighbors and they all awaited Hazel's arrival. Lina had already told Papa Alec Hazel was no longer allowed in her home and she wanted her gone before morning. There was no reasoning with Lina when she was angry.

Papa Alec met Hazel on the bottom steps as she approached. He looked worn out, sad, and much older than a man of his age. It appeared he might have been crying because his eyes were bloodshot and his face redder than usual. Hazel ran to him and stopped suddenly when she noticed his expression. His mouth was moving, and Hazel knew her grandfather was saying something, but she could not hear him. His voice was muffled and practically drowned out by the clanging sound of dishes smashing. This racket was coming from inside the house. As Hazel stood on the steps trying to read Papa Alec's lips, the screaming of a baby started to blend into the smashes. The volume of cries increased as the smashes diminished. It was Abenia crying and without hesitation, Hazel pushed pass Papa Alec to run up the steps causing him to stumble onto the railing. When Hazel reached the front door, Lina was standing there. She was heaving, eyes bulging, her rusty hair that normally would not have a strand out of place was tossed and disheveled on the top of her head. Hazel knew she was no match for Lina even with the age difference, Lina's strength was empowered by her crudeness.

Hazel's heart beat rapidly feeling the thumps vibrating in her throat. Her hands were quivering so much she clutched them together at the base of her back in an attempt to steady herself as she faced Lina. She was scared, almost as fearful as that night in the barn, but this time she had to be strong for her daughter. Papa Alec said nothing as the two women in his life stood motionless. Lina broke the silence when she yelled at Hazel to get off her property and swung the screen door open.

Hazel jumped back to avoid getting hit by the door. Lina kept yelling, this time obscenities as she cornered Hazel on the porch. Hazel could see the shotgun leaning against a pillar. Papa Alec must have left it there after his weekly cleaning. Hazel grabbed the shotgun just as Lina shoved her and she lost her footing. She held the shotgun up pointing towards the top of the porch and fired. The blast was loud causing the floor to shake.

For the first time, Lina did not seem so powerful or in control. Papa Alec lunged himself between the two of them and shouted at Hazel to put the gun down. Hazel was now pointing the barrel directly at Lina's protruding gut. Tears streamed down her cheeks and so did the blood from her bottom lip that was bitten during the blast. At this moment Hazel knew she could shoot and kill Lina. The shotgun felt light in her hands as she aimed it steadily at the indented shadow of Lina's belly button showing through her dress. Memories of mistreatment for years at the hands of Lina filled Hazel's mind like a reservoir over-flooding an embankment.

There was no way to stop the stream as the pressure from her finger built on the trigger. Hazel was in a trance and did not feel Papa Alec reach around her waist to grab the rifle from her hands. Lina ran into the house as Hazel and Papa Alec tussled, both holding onto a portion of the shotgun. Hazel was not able to maintain her grip and soon released her hands giving Papa Alec control. He pleaded over and over with Hazel to leave, promising to look after Abenia until she was settled and able to care for her. Hazel knew she could not stay another second on that farm without harming Lina, and with the few dollars, Papa Alec handed her in one of his handkerchiefs she boarded the Greyhound in Richmond to New York.

~

CHAPTER 2
HARLEM NEW YORK

Rose was wearing her work uniform; a simple white dress, matching stockings and comfortable shoes. She sat on a wooden bench facing the entrance for passengers at the bus station in New York City. She held the telegram in her left hand which was received two days prior from her favorite niece Hazel. They were more like sisters, especially since the age difference was minor. Rose was strikingly beautiful with dark mocha skin, small in stature, shapely in the wanted places, with shoulder-length black hair that was pinned up under a hat today.

She was relieved Hazel was finally joining her and baby brother Red in Harlem. Rose had insisted Hazel leave Lancaster County in the frequent letters she wrote her but was unaware if Lina was intercepting them. Red, whose full name was William Taft Gordon, was not a tall man.

He had fair olive complexion, a chiseled jaw, and wavy hair that could make you seasick if you stared too long. His hair was the color of copper and when the sun shined its rays upon him it looked more like the color of Red, which is how he got his name. He was a handsome man and some folks thought he could pass, which some people of color were doing when they migrated north.

Although Red looked a lot like Papa Alec whose family lineage was from Ireland, he identified more with his mother Nora who was Black. Rose and Red were too familiar with Lina's wrath and were heartbroken with their father's inability to intercede when they were being mistreated. As a boy, Red could never accept that his mother, Nora, left, and so he would run away every chance he got in hopes to find her. He found himself looking for Nora's smile in the faces of all the brown women he passed on the street when in town.

Papa Alec would drag Red back home when he was located, and Lina didn't waste any time beating him with her cane. Lina was angry Red didn't acknowledge her as his mother and would tell him Nora was an unfit mother who ran off with another man. Some years later while cleaning Papa Alec's truck, Hazel accidentally found legal papers to dispute Lina's claim about

Nora and confirmed Lina and her family were responsible for Nora's disappearance. They arranged to have her committed to a mental facility after she had an emotional breakdown. Nora had a delicate temperament and was soft spoken. Sadly, life on the farm was tedious for her and along with raising small children, she was overwhelmed causing her to experience episodes of depression. Lina always had her eye on Papa Alec whenever their paths crossed in Lancaster. Lina saw Nora's condition as an opportunity to ease her way into his life with the bonus of her family taking over the farm. Sweet Nora died in a mental facility only a few miles from the farm and never had the opportunity to reconnect with her children.

Red loved to dance, especially tap dancing. During Sunday church service he couldn't stop his feet from moving when the choir performed. He imagined himself performing on a stage in New York City as he eavesdropped on the conversations held in the parlor when Lina was entertaining. Red learned how good colored folks were doing up north and all the opportunities that were available. He was sure moving to New York he could achieve his dreams and create a life for himself.

Saying goodbye to Hazel was not easy, but he also could not endure another minute under the same roof as Lina. He had lost all respect for Papa Alec too. Red took the first thing smoking out of Virginia one sunny afternoon after church. Red and Rose left the family farm just as soon as they saved enough money for bus fare. They each did jobs and earned a small amount of money sewing and cleaning for some of the church members. On this day, Red was instructed again to remove his "good clothes" which consisted of pants that fit, shoes with sturdy heels and laces, and a shirt that had all the buttons. These directions were accompanied with a smack of Lina's cane upside his head. The beatings occurred weekly and only increased in severity as he got older.

It was Lina's way to dress the children extra nice for church and get the accolades from the congregation on how well she kept them. They were immediately forced to change back into the raggedy garments they wore on the farm and in school. It was shameful how horrible the children looked walking to and from school daily. Rose did her best as a big sister to deter the abuse Lina inflicted upon Red but was met with the same thing if she was too outspoken or visible. Nora's children learned at a young age how to fade into the drapes, carpet, and furnishings in Lina's house to survive.

Hazel arrived in Harlem with a small satchel that wasn't even big enough to hold a hairbrush. She was worn out from not getting any sleep for two days, hungry and frightened. Leaving the only home, she had known, and her daughter caused her heart to ache. She had nothing but the clothes on her back. Hazel had no choice but to believe Papa Alec would keep his word and look after Abenia until she could retrieve her.

Rose greeted Hazel with a warm hug and handed her a paper bag with a sandwich and an apple inside. As they left the station Hazel ate quickly not wanting to appear greedy. She took small bites but chewed fast. Rose could see how distraught Hazel was and decided not to talk about the incident with Lina. She knew it had to be very bad if Hazel left without Abenia.

They walked a while before boarding a bus that took them into Harlem. Rose and Red lived in a small three-story walk-up apartment on Nicholas Avenue. They didn't have many furnishings, but the room was neatly decorated with long brocade drapes at the living room windows, two upholstered wingback chairs, and a scalloped settee in the corner. Rose was a gifted seamstress and created many of the pieces. She made her living sewing and cleaning houses for the wealthy white people who resided on the Upper East Side of the city. Rose acquired these skills reluctantly at an early age while living with Lina when she was forced to do the mending and house chores.

The streets of Harlem were lined with people dressed in fine clothes, busy shops, and decorated eateries. Hazel had never seen so many sophisticated looking colored folks in one place and soon felt a sense of calmness amid all the bustling. She was happy to be with Rose and Red in this magical city. She knew, with all her uncertainties, she could make a life for herself and Abenia away from Lancaster and Lina.

It didn't take Hazel long to acquire a job at a local garment shop stitching lace on fancy undergarments for the sophisticated ladies who frequented the social clubs on Friday nights. Red was able to live out his passion performing his dance routines along with three other handsome guys on a makeshift stage created by the shop's owner to entertain patron's after hours. Red later became a member of a dance group called the "Four Step Brothers" who were famous in Harlem and performed around the world wearing tuxedos and tapping shoes. Many of the shop owners in Harlem utilized their establishments for multiple purposes as a resource for additional money. It wasn't unusual for an eatery to serve breakfast and lunch until 3 pm and reopen at 8 pm as a dance hall equipped with a live band, singers and performers. The nightlife in Harlem was filled with zest and vigor along with a commonality of self-love amongst the people that lived there. It was a place that exuded beauty and confidence. Residents of this charming borough worked hard all week in many capacities ranging from doctors to domestics. At night they were carefree folks who in smoked filled rooms mingled, danced lively, and lost track of time captured in the Harlem Renaissance.

Hazel saved most of her small earnings as a seamstress towards her goal of retrieving her daughter from Lancaster. She also worked part-time cleaning houses and cooking for wealthy families in New York. Aunt Rose was already employed as a domestic for several families and was able to recommend Hazel when additional help was needed. Normally, this was for dinner parties, family gatherings, and religious events. Both Gordon women were more than familiar with culinary and domestic duties after all the years maintaining the services required by Lina. Being of servitude to Lina and her family were not memories they could shake; however, at least they were now getting paid.

Hazel wanted to keep busy. It was a way to occupy her thoughts and distract the yearning for her baby girl. Rose and Red did their best by insisting Hazel join them when they hit the town at night. Hazel became fond of jazz after seeing Duke

Ellington perform at the Cotton Club. Cab Calloway was also a regular and she even cut a rug on the dance floor when he belted, 'Hi de Hi de Ho' during a sold-out performance. Harlem at this time was the best place to be for colored folks, especially those in need of a change from the south. Several months had passed, and Hazel remained in Harlem.

Red was now in the military and had been shipped to Alaska to join the US Troops working on the Alaskan Pipeline. He wrote about the horrible issues he was having with his feet in the freezing cold and how he didn't think he would be able to dance again when he returned. Rose missed her baby brother and worried about his well-being. She had always protected Red when they were growing up; shielding him from Lina's rage and making excuses for him when he misbehaved. She felt helpless and like Hazel immersed herself in her daily work duties to divert her thoughts.

Rose also had no problem attracting gentlemen callers who were more than happy to take her dancing most evenings. On one occasion she encouraged Hazel to join her at the Savoy and the famous boxer, Joe Louis, came in with an entourage. After being seated the 'Brown Bomber,' as he was called, noticed Hazel who was seated with Rose and her companion at a nearby table.

He came over to introduce himself to her but was hesitant after Hazel didn't seem phased with his notoriety. Apparently, Hazel had very similar features to the boxer's current girlfriend which must have perked his interest. Although this was a fleeting moment Hazel encountered, she couldn't wait to write Red and share the news about her almost date with Joe Louis. Years later Hazel would jokingly share that she could have married Joe Louis since she looked like his wife. These fun times of harmless flirting with celebrities felt good.

While in Lancaster, Hazel never had the opportunity to flirt, dance or even converse with boys. Sharing an evening out getting lost in the soulful sounds of Jazz with Rose and her suitors were also welcome distractions.

Hazel kept reassuring herself that Abenia was fine on the farm. Whenever a bad thought crossed her mind of what could be, she quickly dismissed it. It was becoming harder for Hazel to dispel these haunting thoughts. Finally, she asked her Aunt Rose to send a letter to Papa Alec to inquire about Abenia because she couldn't. Hazel vowed she would never have anything else to do with Papa Alec, step foot on that farm again, or even attend her grandfather's funeral when he died. Hazel managed to keep all those promises.

It was almost a month since the letter was sent to Papa Alec before Rose received a response. Rose didn't recognize the handwriting at first; it had been a long time since she saw her father's writing. The envelope was smudged with what appeared to be soot. She imagined he addressed the envelope after tending to the fireplace in the parlor. It wasn't a full written letter but a scripted folded note with eight words. "The little girl is dead. She had consumption," signed Papa.

Hazel spent the rest of the month in a mental stupor. She kept reliving the last time she saw her beautiful baby girl. How she inhaled one last smell from the crevice of her neck. Abenia was strong and healthy, so full of life. It was inconceivable that she was gone, and Hazel would never see her again. Why didn't Papa Alec write when it happened? Was he instructed by Lina not to tell? The unanswered questions consumed her, and she blamed herself for not being with Abenia when she took ill and passed.

Rose didn't have any children of her own, but she understood loss. The feeling of helplessness and regret. She harbored those same emotions towards her mother, Nora. As a young woman in Lancaster, it was overwhelming at times, even more so after she found out the true cause for her mother's leaving. Consoling Hazel with her presence was all Rose could do. She sat up with her at night when all Hazel did was whimper, no words or outwardly cries, just long and slow whimpers. Her heart was wounded, but so was her spirit, her purpose, and drive. Abenia was the only reason she woke up at the crack of dawn for work every day and sewed until her hands ached until the sunset had vanished.

There was no going back to Lancaster for Hazel to say her final goodbye at a funeral or bury her baby girl at the end of the farm where the trees lined up almost in a single formation; which was not far from where Papa Alec laid Trixie to rest. Hazel kept her promise to never set foot on that land again as long as she lived, so Rose offered to travel to Virginia and speak directly with Papa Alec. He was her father and part of her hoped since so much time had passed, things between them would be different. She had not seen Papa Alec or Lancaster in years. Rose missed the unpaved roads, the luscious green grass that covered the farms and fields, the smell of honeysuckle from the trees when the wind blows. It was home in spite of the privations the Gordon children experienced while living there. Rose didn't want to just show up on the farm without notice. She knew Lina would not welcome her arrival. Lina was adamant about Rose not returning, just like she was with Red and Hazel when they decided to leave.

Hazel, riddled with grief, managed to give herself a bird bath, put on a dress, and brushed her hair into a bun that rested at the nape of her neck. It was almost seven weeks since she got the news about her daughter's death. She didn't even have a photo of her baby girl; only a few ribbons that she had used in her hair. Hazel kept them wrapped inside the same handkerchief Papa Alec gave her when she left Lancaster. She mourned in silence the life she dreamt about creating for herself and Abenia. But honestly, a part of her felt a sense of relief that Abenia was no longer with Lina. Though this feeling disturbed Hazel, she accepted this truth and it empowered her to move on with her life.

Rose arrived in Virginia on a balmy summer day. She stood outside the church she attended as a child swatting away flies with her small purse. Papa Alec agreed to meet her there on his way to the oyster plant. It was decided to keep her arrival a secret from Lina; therefore, a visit to the farm was out of the question. She wanted to see it one more time. Perhaps, to make sure it was still real. She also wanted to make sure Lina saw that her premonitions and rants of failure did not come true. But her childlike fear remained, and this time Papa Alec made a decision that she thought was in her best interest.

The town folk didn't recognize Rose dressed in her pale blue dress with matching color pin hat sitting low on the front of her head. She made it a point to wear her best attire and it was also one of a kind that she designed and created herself. Rose noticed Papa Alec from a distance his steel gray eyes had softened with age and his straight-as-a pole stature was more like a bent tree limb now. His stride was slower as he approached, still wearing his lucky fishing hat that had more holes than fabric. He seemed happy to see Rose, or it could have been her wishful thinking. Nonetheless, her father was standing right in front of her and that was more than a wish it was a dream come true. She wanted to hug him longer, but he released his grip hurriedly and she obliged not to seem needy. They stood in front of the old church for what felt like an hour, but it was only fifteen minutes.

Before she could ask, he blurted, "There was nothing more I could do for Hazel's daughter; she's gone."

He turned and as he walked away, he said, "I am sorry Rose, sorry for everything." The flies suddenly were still just like Rose as she stood motionless watching her father disappear as he turned the corner. Her feet felt heavy as lead when she tried to take a step. She knew she had to move, or she would surely topple over. Sweat melted down her face and trickled in the middle of her back. She didn't want to appear shaken or upset, but she was completely out of sorts by his callousness. Rose knew she needed to leave Lancaster immediately and accept that this was probably the last time she would see her father.

Harlem had become a haven for Hazel as she began to build a future. Her days continued to be busy tending to the homes of wealthy people and most evenings she frequented the lively night clubs with Rose. She didn't drink much, but she certainly loved to dance. Much like Red, she found dance as an escape. While dancing she felt present in the moment. Each wavering movement of her arms and feet released bits of sorrow into the universe that could be swallowed whole. There were no rules when dancing; you just blended in on the floor and let the sounds of the music guide you. These nightly jaunts of dance made Hazel's heartache a little easier to live with.

~

CHAPTER 3
ASBURY PARK NEW JERSEY

They were fortunate to hear domestic workers were needed at some of the fancy hotels on the seashore in the summer. Rose suggested she and Hazel take a trip to a quaint town called Asbury Park, New Jersey. Neither one of them had ever been to the Jersey Shore or any other beach for that matter. Rose thought the sea, sun, and extra money would be a welcome change for them. Hazel and Rose decided to take the noon train out of Grand Central Station in midtown New York. This enabled them to arrive at the Asbury Park train station before 3 o'clock pm.

The train station at the resort shore town was a short walking distance away from the historic boardwalk with the miles of wooden planks and close-up views of the enchanted Atlantic Ocean. They had plenty of time to stroll the infamous boardwalk and ogle at the sights of the lavish hotels that nestled along the sea's border. They were staying at a rooming house in town and the check-in time was 7 pm. The rooming house was located on the East Side of Asbury Park just a few blocks from the beach. Many of the vintage Victorian houses with large wrap around porches in this area were designated during the season for the summer domestic shore workers. A nominal weekly fee covered the room accommodations which included two twin beds, a small basin, and a light daily breakfast. The morning breakfast consisted of freshly baked rolls with a bowl of seasonal fruit, all prepared by the owner, Mrs. Sophia.

Mrs. Sophia owned one of the Victorian houses on 7th Avenue. It had six large bedrooms, a massive kitchen with a dining area that could seat ten comfortably and a sitting room fit for entertaining. The house resembled something out of a fairy tale with large overgrown rose bushes that draped along the step railings, whimsical figurines of angels adorned the front lawn and bright yellow and light blue awnings hung from the twelve windows on the front of the house. She was a small woman with a strong Italian accent, widowed when her husband Franco was killed in the war. They didn't have children and after his passing, Mrs. Sophia opened her home by offering rooms for people vacationing and visiting the shore. She was one of the first in Asbury Park to extend this courtesy to people of color and was often ridiculed for her choices. Mrs. Sophia did not concern herself with what people thought. She just loved people regardless of where they came from or what color they were.

Her husband Franco felt the same and prior to him leaving home for the army he owned a Bakery and Luncheonette in Belmar, a town south of Asbury Park where he employed people of color full-time. Essentially, Mrs. Sophia knew renting rooms was also a viable resource to acquire income and financial stability on a regular basis.

The steady breeze from the Ocean caused Hazel and Rose to hold onto their hats with the free hand that wasn't clutching their small satchel of clothing as they strolled. They felt an overwhelming sense of bliss but knew they had to be cautious because colored folks were not welcome on the beach or boardwalk every day of the week. It was a Tuesday afternoon and by the looks of others on the boardwalk who were glimpsing at the glistening water, it was not a day for people of color to be strolling. Rose hurried her pace and Hazel followed when they noticed people starting to stare and whisper to each other.

The Royal Hotel would be their working home for the next

six to eight weeks. The building had ten floors with massive windows and towered over all the other small hotel establishments nearby. It was not as elaborate as the newly constructed Bentley Carlson located at the end of the boardwalk, but it held a charm and glamour that welcomed all the occupants. The hired help was not allowed to enter the front entrance past the bellhop workers who parked the cars of the patrons. They were instructed to quietly find the service entrance on the main level located in the back near the garbage containers. Everyone working in the domestic capacity at the Royal Hotel were people of color; mostly black folks who decided to spend their summer at the Jersey Shore away from their homes and families to earn money.

Breakfast at Mrs. Sophia's rooming house was delectable and substantial. She took enormous pride in seeing people enjoy her food. Hazel and Rose wanted to indulge in second helpings especially the homemade rolls with fresh strawberry jam, but they did not want to overeat; unsure of the labor intense responsibilities that awaited them on their first day at the hotel. However, they also needed to ensure they had eaten enough since they didn't know how long it would be before their next meal. Both were also concerned about overspending since the purpose was to save money during their summer work adventure. Purchasing a brownstone in the Strivers Row section of Harlem was a dream of Rose's. She wanted to have a place with her brother Red and now Hazel that they could claim and call home.

They arrived early on their first day at the Royal Hotel, ready to work and begin what would be a summer to remember. Hazel was given the ten rooms on the first floor to dust, sweep, change linens, and towels. Rose was required to do the same tasks on the eighth floor which had eight rooms and a lounge area. Both had to work quickly and not disturb or interrupt the hotel guests. They were given gray short sleeve cotton dresses to wear along with white hair nets. The cleaning supplies were distributed in the basement of the hotel with makeshift baskets to carry to the occupant floors. Comfortable shoes were a must and since they worked domestic jobs in New York it wasn't difficult for them to adapt.

After several hours of working, they were given a half an hour break. During the break, Hazel couldn't wait to see the beach again and insisted they skip eating for a stroll on the boardwalk. Throughout the day Hazel kept looking out the floor-to-ceiling windows in the rooms she was cleaning just to get a small glimpse of a wave rushing to reach the shore. She wanted to recapture the sense of clarity that encased her like a cocoon when the smashing sounds of waves against the sand and the pungent ocean scent of fresh salt collided. Rose agreed but knew tomorrow they had to prepare better by packing lunches for their 'break at the beach' escape. She thought Mrs. Sophia might be inclined to send them off in the morning with an extra hot roll and some of that yummy jam. Rose would ask Mrs. Sophia kindly after she praised her culinary skills. Rose knew a little extra sweet-talking could help her request.

The first couple of weeks working at the Royal Hotel and visiting the Asbury Park shore became a favorable routine for Hazel and Rose. They continued to clean and manage the rooms on their assigned floors, and both were even given extra duties and privileges throughout the hotel that allowed them access to the kitchen and entertainment areas. Hazel had not forgotten her way around the kitchen and was still a wonderful baker and cook. Often, she was asked to assist in the kitchen and was elated to spend extra time with the hotel cooks. They enjoyed sharing recipes and stories.

Some of the kitchen staff were residents of the West Side of Asbury Park, which was primarily people of color. They were intrigued about the happenings in Harlem and asked if Hazel had been to any of the many famous locations. The kitchen workers had heard great things about the Cotton Club, The Savoy, and the eclectic shops on 145th Street. Hazel and Rose willingly shared their adventures in Harlem. Rose with more exhilaration because she truly loved everything about Harlem and felt like a native New Yorker.

Hazel was excited to see the West Side of Asbury Park after their story swapping. Marie, who she met in the kitchen was one of the West Side domestic workers. She was a petite woman with dark brown hair worn tapered at the back with a swoop of hair swirled behind her ear. Her skin looked like a shiny copper penny which enhanced the sparkle of her deep brown eyes. Hazel and Marie had become quite chummy as they laughed and giggled like schoolgirls while baking the apple and peach pies that were favorites of the hotel guest. Hazel never had a true girlfriend and besides Rose, she didn't spend much time with anyone else.

Marie invited Hazel and Rose to a fundraising event at her church. Marie attended Holy Redeemer; the Catholic Church located on the East Side of Asbury Park. However, the people of color attending the church were in the process of establishing their own location on the West Side of town where most of the congregants resided. Marie also offered to give them a grand tour of the West Side, the one-half mile mecca of the city she called home, before the church event.

It was a bright sunny morning perfect for a day of fun and site seeing. They ate assorted salt water taffy from eateries on the boardwalk and laughed until their sides hurt. The ladies anxiously climbed into the swan-like replica paddle boats docked on Wesley Lake near the carousel amusement. Hazel hadn't felt this carefree in a long time; not since her days spent on the farm riding Trixie early mornings before the chores began. She forgot how good it felt to be silly and laugh, even at herself. The lake was calm as they paddled from one side to the other. Beautiful homes with gigantic pillars, luscious green lawns, and wrap around porches with cushioned rattan chairs surrounded their views from the lake.

Hazel tried to imagine the families living in these houses. She wondered if they ate elaborate meals together and later gathered on the porch for dessert. Hazel also speculated if the people in the houses appreciated the beauty that encircled their haven and for a fleeting moment, she missed the farm, but mostly she yearned for the time on the farm with Abenia.

The West Side of Asbury Park was only a few feet from the

lake across the main street of the town. It was separated by the visible boundary of the railroad tracks from the East Side of Asbury Park.

The stroll down Springwood Avenue, the street that connected the different sides of the city was fascinating. It reminded Hazel of Harlem with all the activity and excitement of folks who were mainly people of color. Springwood Avenue was filled with eateries, hair salons, barbershops, tailor shops, churches of various religions on each corner, nightclubs, pool halls, and family-run stores. This West Side jewel of a street created an atmosphere of pride. It was a town within a town where people of color lived and thrived.

There were apartments, homes large and modest, and schools both public and parochial. The streets were wide and clean with concrete sidewalks that looked newly paved. Men dressed in suits nodded and tipped their hats when they passed and women wearing belted skirts or knee-length dresses glanced and smiled. Hazel was a little overwhelmed with how friendly strangers were in this small town but felt this place could be her home away from home.

Marie's church event was a luncheon to raise funds for the new church being built. It was held at the local community center on the West Side where residents frequented for various types of occasions including dances, weddings, and talent shows. Marie showed Hazel and Rose the construction site on the corner of Springwood and Ridge Avenues. There were two buildings on the property. A small tan brick church with steep steps that led to the entrance of two large wooden doors and the rectory residence in the rear that was detached from the church. Both structures were almost completed.

Rose and Hazel attended the Baptist Church in Lancaster with Lina and Papa Alec every Sunday. It was imperative to Lina that they kept up appearances. If the congregation only knew nothing was as it appeared. Since leaving Virginia Rose showed no interest in any organized religion nor was, she in search of any now. Meanwhile, Hazel was more than ready to learn about Marie's faith and welcomed the interaction with church members. She always found a sense of tranquility in church and felt closer to God when she was there. After leaving the church in Lancaster shamed and disheartened, Hazel's hopes of finding that fulfillment again were fleeting. Marie's enthusiasm when she spoke of her church home and how connected they were with the community touched Hazel.

They arrived at the community center just in time to locate

seats next to each other, The tables were decorated with glass vases filled with daisies, white linen and floral plates. There was a mixed crowd of couples young and old and many were closer to Hazel's age. After sitting for a few minutes, Marie excused herself to go help with some of the other church ladies in the kitchen area. They were organizing the food on platters and cutting the pies and cakes into small slices. Hazel was glad her Aunt Rose was with her since they didn't know anyone else there except Marie.

The room filled quickly and soon members of the church started to come over to greet Hazel and Rose and introduce themselves. Everyone seemed nice, friendly and eager to converse. Most wanted to know if Rose and Hazel enjoyed the boardwalk, working in the hotel and if they planned to stay in the city of Asbury Park.

Marie rejoined them at the table before the program started. She told Hazel that one of the elders of the church approached her while she was in the kitchen helping. The elder asked if she could introduce her son to Hazel when he came to pick her up. Hazel was surprised with the woman's request and was unaware she had been seen. Apparently, Mrs. Maggie Walker noticed Hazel and Rose when they came into the community center.

Marie knew Daniel because he attended church with his mother and father every Sunday. He was a stout man of average height, brown skin with a pronounced nose. He always smiled and was polite whenever they saw each other and exchanged pleasantries. Daniel wasn't bad to look at and some would say he was handsome. He was attentive to his parents and seemed like the type of man that would be loyal. She knew he worked at one of the greasy spoon establishments in town and part-time at HANKS Stop-Hop in Belmar both as a short order cook. Marie heard Daniel also aspired to start a janitorial business one day.

Hazel was not interested in meeting anyone romantically and was reluctant to get acquainted with any man. She never truly dated or had any genuine gentlemen callers. Her experiences with men were tainted with distrust and heartache based on her history in Lancaster.

Hazel felt it was impossible to erase her past, but she also knew in order to move on she had to take chances, just like when she left Lancaster and moved to Harlem. Now, the chance she was taking was to meet Daniel Howard Lee Walker.

QUOTE

"STOP TO THINK

AND YOU MAY THINK TO STOP."

- HAZEL GORDON WALKER

~

CHAPTER 4
AQUAINTANCE

Their first encounter was a greeting arranged by relatives and friends who thought two single people might make a connection. Hazel was numb when it came to her feelings. Opening her heart right now meant being vulnerable and she wasn't prepared for that. After attending the church fundraiser with Rose and Marie, Hazel immersed herself in her duties as a domestic worker at the Royal Hotel.

When busy working, Hazel was most at ease. It was second nature to assist with the additional chores in the hotel kitchen when she was done with cleaning her assigned rooms. Hazel had a staunch work ethic, something she was accustomed to from living on a farm in Lancaster. Often, she would help other workers when needed and join Rose and Marie for a stroll on the boardwalk when time permitted. Meeting Daniel was an unexpected snag in her pattern of things and initially, she didn't find it instructive. She was managing her life okay with the occasional outing with Marie and Rose to the TURF Lounge on the West Side to see performers like Lena Horne and Count Basie.

The musicians and singers would stop by many of the shore clubs after a show in Harlem. It was a surprise each week to see who would show up. These spontaneous performances were similar to the nightlife in Harlem and they were entertaining. Rose really missed Harlem and wanted to get back there as soon as the summer job was over. She hoped Red would also be home from his military tour in Alaska and they could resume their lives as a family again. Meanwhile, Hazel was enamored with the town of Asbury Park and began to visualize herself as a resident.

Daniel, an only child, lived with his parents, Morton and Maggie, in a two-story house they owned on a quiet street lined with tall trees, full hedges and manicured lawns. It was a racially mixed neighborhood comprised of working-class blacks and some Italians on the West Side of Asbury Park in the late 1920s and 1930s. Many spent their week working or managing the local establishments in town, while some traveled to surrounding areas to work the farms, and on the weekend, they went to church. Everyone had a vested interest in the community and took pride in maintaining their properties.

Morton originally from St. George County Maryland was a tall thin stylish man with a striking stern face that matched his demeanor. He had strong big hands and a confidence that made people cower. Most would consider him a man with a mean temperament and dominating presence. Morton was aloof in nature and showed minimum interest in what people thought. With no formal education, Morton worked labor intensive jobs as a farm worker and groundskeeper in the town of Freehold to support his family. He walked miles to work every day leaving home before the sun came up and returning when the stars lit up the streets paving his way back. He cherished his money and was reluctant to spend it on any luxuries except chewing tobacco, hats, and suits. Weekly, he gave his entire pay to his wife and only requested spending money on Saturday evenings when he attended a card game. Rumors of Morton spending time with other ladies in town surfaced, but none were substantiated.

Maggie, quite the opposite of her husband, was short, and pleasingly plump with an infectious loud laugh. She gave big hugs and loved to cook.

She acquired limited formal education growing up in rural North Carolina. She migrated to Asbury Park along with her sisters to work as domestics in the homes of affluent white people. Maggie's dream after arriving in town was to own a home and fill it with all the amenities like her privileged employers. She loved fine china, heavy damask drapes, and leaded crystal.

Maggie and Morton believed with hard work anything was possible. Their lives were reminiscent of many folks of color on the West Side who were the once removed generation from slavery and now living the dream their ancestors only imagined.

Hazel and Rose spent a great deal of time with Marie on their days off, enjoying all the exciting aspects of the city. They understood why Marie and the other locals loved Asbury Park after they became acquainted with the resort town. Hazel was especially drawn to Marie's church and its valued presence in the community. The church services were not like what she was accustomed to in Lancaster. They were different in many ways. In Marie's church, the services were reserved and extremely structured. The congregants spent minimum time chatting and more time praying. Although, everyone was friendly and greeted each other the services lasted approximately an hour and people were on their way. Hazel felt comfortable worshipping there and looked forward to attending church each week. Daniel along with his parents Morton and Maggie were always in the front row with many of the other faithful members. Soon some of the congregants would be attending the newly built church on the West Side with its wooden pews, stained glass windows, and 20-foot high peaked ceilings. It was small compared to Holy Redeemer, their current church with its massive brick pillars and grand alter, but it was large in connectedness.

Maggie had happily introduced Hazel to Daniel after the luncheon weeks earlier and would instigate interactions whenever she had the opportunity at church. Marie and Rose also encouraged their union and even suggested Hazel look for permanent employment in one of the large houses on the East Side of the city. She was a dependable worker and received numerous accolades about her work at the Royal Hotel. They were also certain Maggie would assist without any hesitation, especially since she was currently working as the primary housekeeper for a wealthy well-known family in the city.

The beach and boardwalk were sparse with people now and occupants in the hotels on the shore were dwindling down. Children were heard complaining about returning to school as cars were loaded with luggage and seashore memorabilia.

It was a clear sign summer was ending, along with their engaging jobs at the hotel and Rose was eagerly awaiting her return to treasured Harlem. However, Hazel, although fond of Harlem was keeping her options open. Hazel felt she had nothing to lose and was secretly excited about possibly starting a new life in Asbury Park.

~

CHAPTER 5
CONNECTION

Red never had the opportunity to tap dance again with the 'Four Step Brothers' or any other dance group. Hazel remembered how much he loved to perform as a young boy and how he fantasized about going to New York where he could make his dream a reality. She was happy he was able to achieve so many of his aspirations, even if it was short lived.

At the funeral, Hazel couldn't help but wonder if Red had made up with Papa Alec on the other side. Sadly, they did not reconnect or see each other again after he ran off to New York. It was rumored Papa Alec died a few months after his encounter with Rose in Lancaster leaving his offspring an irresoluble legacy. Hazel hoped Red had healed feet, new dancing shoes and was tapping all over heaven. He suffered so much after his honorable discharge from the military and ended up in a VA Hospital in his final days. Rose always the strong one was called to identify Red's body after his passing and privately said goodbye to her baby brother. After the funeral Red did make it back to Virginia and was buried in the notable Arlington Cemetery along with so many other worthy soldiers.

Hazel returned to Harlem with Rose. She briefly reconsidered her decision to marry Daniel and move to Asbury Park. Hazel was nervous about living with his parents, especially Morton who did not seem thrilled about their planned nuptials. Daniel was an only child and she could understand his parent's apprehension. He did not have a steady full-time job that would afford him the ability to provide for his wife and any children they may have. Morton did not consider Daniel working part-time as a short order cook at eateries a stable means of employment. He wanted Daniel to join the military or obtain an office job since he did have the smarts.

The teachers at the local Catholic high school Daniel attended expressed how his intellect exceeded many of his classmates. He was excellent with numbers and could read anything he got his hands on; books, newspapers, box cartons, you name it, Daniel would read it. However, even with his thirst for knowledge and mathematical skills Daniel was not highly motivated to expand his scope of prospective employers and was happy with his current positions.

Hazel and Daniel were married in the fall of 1931 at Holy Redeemer Church in Asbury Park. It was a clear day without a cloud in the sky. A significant amount of colorful leaves had fallen from trees and lined the sidewalks. There was a slight breeze felt from the ocean nearby. Hazel wore a navy-blue dress with full pleated sleeves that tapered from the elbow down to her wrist. The bottom skirt had a fitted band that accented her tiny waist and flowed lightly down to her ankles. Daniel was cleanly shaven except for his pencil mustache. He was handsome not like Duke or Joe, but attractive. He wore a matching navy suit with a tie he borrowed from his father's collection. Marie and Daniel's Uncle Lawrence stood with them as their maid of honor and best man. Uncle Lawrence was married to Fannie, Morton's sister.

It was a simple wedding performed by the priest right before the 9 o'clock mass. Rose along with her new suitor, Alfred, a man she met waiting in line at a movie theater in Harlem, sat in the front pew along with Daniel's parents Morton and Maggie. Alfred a tall thin man with dark eyes and thick hair worked on the railroad. He was originally from Arlington, Virginia and owned a home there that he inherited from his family. Rose experienced a sense of relief when Hazel said, "I do" and although she knew Daniel wasn't exactly what Hazel had imagined as a husband, she knew he was kind, loyal and not mean spirited. She hoped Hazel would find joy in her new life.

The Walker house at 208 Elizabeth Avenue was surrounded with large baby blue hydrangea bushes. They hung over the railings leading up the steps to the wide front porch. The backyard was narrow but long and finely manicured. In the summer large plump grapes were a welcome treat from the grapevines that separated the neighbors. The West Side neighborhood consisted of bungalows and two-story colonials. Most had full basements and spacious yards.

It was racially diverse with first-and second-generation Italian families and Black families who migrated from the south. Everyone was amicable and often shared cups of sugar and stories while gathered on their large porches. The churches, Baptist, Catholic, Episcopal, Methodist, were in walking distance and the local shops were frequented by all who resided on the West Side. Most folks kept a running tab at Mr. Ravens the go-to shop for everything from bread to buttons and settled their accounts on payday. Many West Side residents used the *'shoe sole express'* to travel to and from destinations in town. Morton and Maggie did not own a car and neither ever learned how to drive. Daniel continued that same mode of transportation and Hazel did too when she joined the family.

The house appeared large with three bedrooms occupying the second floor for sleeping and one bathroom with a claw foot tub, porcelain round sink and toilet on the same level. The Walker's did not share a bedroom, Hazel found that odd since other married people she knew slept in the same room. Maggie's bedroom was in the front part of the house. It was filled with large antique furnishings; a grand chifforobe, a full-size dark wooden poster bed, and a scalloped mirrored vanity with a matching chair. Mornings, after preparing breakfast and before Mass, Maggie sat at the wood carved vanity and applied her favorite lavender perfume.

Morton's bedroom was right next door to Maggie's. It was much smaller with a dresser drawer and a twin-size bed adorned with a heavy striped quilt neatly folded at the foot. The closet was filled with matching suits, starched button-down shirts, and various fedora hats. Morton was a sharp dresser. He took great pride in making sure he looked his best from head to toe. His shoes had to be spit-shined, shirt collars starched, and suit pants were creased.

Hazel and Daniel slept in the third bedroom located beside the bathroom at the top of the wooden stairwell. The room was similar in size to Morton's except it was large enough to hold a full-size bed and a narrow satin settee. It was sparsely decorated with a tiny closet and a hook on the back of the door to hold a coat. Hazel had acquired quite a wardrobe from Rose's seamstress talents and could not imagine where she would keep her belongings. She hoped there would be space available elsewhere in the house.

The first level of the house had a cozy living room as you entered with a large tan upholstered sofa and two matching armed chairs. Heavy olive-green drapes adorned the dual windows on each side of the beveled glass entrance door. A large oak bookcase sat in the far corner along with a floor to ceiling black enamel lamp with long gold stems and adjustable shades. The dining room was filled with beautiful mahogany furnishings a bit oversized for the room and somewhat extravagant, but Maggie couldn't say no when she was offered the hand-me-downs from her employers when they redecorated.

At the back of the house was the checkered floor kitchen large enough for a full wooden table and chairs, white glass covered cabinets, and a stocked pantry with an icebox. Access to the full basement was from the kitchen which held wooden shelves on a wall with jars of various preserves, extra linen, and quilts. The basement had a double concrete basin with a washboard and a clothesline that hung overhead. Outside the entry were two red hinged cellar doors leading to the fenced back yard. Maggie, a maid, and Morton, a laborer, were proud homeowners who took great care of their property.

Hazel settled into her new life as Daniel's wife on Elizabeth Avenue and kept herself busy baking, cooking and assisting with the household chores. She also worked days as the first-floor maid for a family her mother-in-law had suggested on the East Side of town. Daniel continued working as a short order cook at the restaurant in Belmar, but also started doing janitorial work at the Catholic high school he graduated from.

Hazel frequently caught the train to visit Rose in Harlem when she didn't have to work. They enjoyed spending time perusing Harlem and catching up on their lives. Rose was now engaged to Alfred and planned on relocating to Virginia after they married. He had taken a long-term assignment in New York but didn't want to settle there. Rose and Alfred also spent long weekends in Asbury Park and hung out with Hazel and Marie at the local movie theaters, restaurants, and jazz clubs. There were scads of entertainment in town for people of color.

Daniel never joined them on these excursions and spent most of his free time at the pool hall on Springwood Avenue. He didn't spend much money, but he enjoyed a friendly card game. Daniel also began doing the bookkeeping for the numbers racket that was being secretly run out of the establishment. There wasn't much money passed his way, but he liked numbers, he always did, and he also felt a sense of importance amongst the guys that gathered there.

~

CHAPTER 6
HOME

Four years into the marriage and still residing with Daniel's parents, Hazel received a letter from Rose summarizing correspondence, she had recently read from a relative. Uncle Tommy, who resided in Maryland, was complaining about the hardship his sister Addie was having trying to provide for her family. Apparently, Aunt Addie's husband passed away suddenly, and she was left with the responsibility of raising six children. Uncle Tommy said Addie was barely able to keep the kids clothed and food on the table. He expressed how selfish it was to expect Addie to take care of someone else's child. He ended the letter stating, "Hazel needs to come and get her daughter."

Hazel promptly boarded the train into New York to speak with Rose directly about the letter from Uncle Tommy. She knew it had to be a mistake or some confusion about Addie's circumstance. Once again, Rose offered to intercede and travel south to visit Aunt Addie to see for herself what child Uncle Tommy was talking about. Now, more than ever, Hazel appreciated Rose's ability to face interactions. She couldn't leave Asbury Park on short notice or explain an unexpected trip to Maryland to Daniel or her prying in-laws. Hazel imagined this child Uncle Tommy spoke of must be one of her mother's, Julia, who was also living in Maryland. Rose agreed that Hazel's assumption made sense but still wanted to find out for herself.

Rose packed a small bag with minimum essentials, bundled up with warm clothing since it was winter, and traveled to Maryland with her fiancé, Alfred. He didn't mind driving even at night. Alfred was up and down the roadway more frequently now, after he and Rose got engaged. He hoped they would be settled in Virginia soon and all this traveling would be behind him.

The dirt road leading to Aunt Addie's house was rocky with large crevices that swallowed your tires. Alfred was sure the axel on the car would be blown by the time they pulled up to the house. Rose jumped out of the car and quickly ran to the front door. Alfred sat for a while with the engine running before joining her. The house felt damp and Aunt Addie looked frail and frazzled as children of various ages ran amok from the kitchen to the sitting room. It was a small bungalow with bright blue painted walls and worn furnishings. Rose looked closely at the children as they breezed by knocking and stumbling into each other. She was hoping to see Julia's double in the face of one of the little girls, but as one of the tiny doll-like figures with auburn hair stopped suddenly at her feet it was Hazel's eyes that stared back at her.

Alfred, who is usually a quiet man, made a loud squeal when he saw the little girl staring at Rose. She looked remarkably like Hazel; there was no denying Uncle Tommy was right.

Aunt Addie then began to tell Rose that Lina wanted no parts of Abenia shortly after Hazel took off. She wasn't aware of the true reason Hazel left the farm and obviously no one volunteered to tell her any of the goings on there. She went on to say Papa Alec would drop off clothes and a little money for Abenia from time to time, but that stopped soon after he passed away. Rose was furious her father lied about Abenia for so long and that he would deliberately cause Hazel additional pain. There was no longer a need to forgive him or make excuses for his dreadful behavior because he was dead and right now Rose was angry.

After a few hours visiting, Alfred and Rose headed back to

Virginia. Aunt Addie was reluctant about them taking Abenia, but she also knew she was not in a position to provide much and thought the child should be with her mother.

Abenia fell asleep in the back seat soon after they drove onto Highway 95. She didn't even ask where they were going, and Rose thought she appeared to be relieved to leave Maryland. They stopped on the way for a quick bathroom break and some needed snacks. They didn't have anything to eat while at Addie's house and everyone was now hungry. Rose also took this opportunity to send Hazel a message via a telegram to let her know she would be back in New York by the weekend and that she needed to be there when she arrived. It was already Wednesday, and Alfred had to go back to work on Friday.

Rose felt nervous about returning with Abenia, but also ecstatic that Hazel would have her little girl back. She wasn't sure how this new revelation would affect their lives and wondered if Hazel's new family would accept her daughter. Daniel was not aware of Hazel's past nor that she had given birth to a child. She didn't share this information with him or any of her new acquaintances in Harlem or Asbury Park. Rose knew after Hazel lost Abenia it was a difficult time in her life, and she did not want to conjure up those sad emotions.

Daniel was busy working the part-time evening shift doing janitorial service in Belmar and was spending most of his days writing the numbers at the local pool hall on the avenue. He didn't seem interested in pursuing other viable and stable means of employment. One of his classmates from high school set him up with a position in the accounting department at Fort Monmouth, the military base located about five towns north of Asbury Park. Many of the local guys were securing good paying jobs there with excellent benefits. Everyone knew Daniel was a wiz with numbers and his buddy figured since he was married now and would most likely start a family soon this would be a great opportunity.

Daniel had other ideas on how he wanted to earn money. Shockingly, he declined the assistance without considering the positive impact this position would have for his family. Hazel was disappointed with his decision and started to resent his aimless behavior. Every day she worked cleaning houses and cooking for other families and still managed to assist Daniel's mother with the same chores when she got home. Hazel felt this was reminiscent of the life she lived in Lancaster; except now the treatment was in the form of broken promises and selfishness. She thought of leaving the marriage since they did not have any children yet, but her faith and a yearning for a family kept her there.

Hazel arrived at the apartment in Harlem early Friday morning. She was on the train before the sun came up, but still managed to fix breakfast for Daniel and Morton before walking downtown. She asked her friend Marie to cover for her that weekend at work. Marie took care of the Larrington family household which was a few houses down from where Hazel's employers lived. Marie would have to stay late on those days juggling the two homes, but she knew how important this trip to New York was to Hazel. They were all anxiously awaiting the news Rose had to tell about her trip to Maryland.

Hazel noticed Alfred's car was parked in front of the apartment. He must have been tired when they arrived in Harlem last night because the back end of the car was sticking out onto the street; not evenly in the parking space like usual. Rose was still asleep when Hazel opened the door to the apartment. Hazel still had her key and offered to return it when Alfred started staying there when in town, but Rose insisted she keep it for emergencies. The living room had not changed much since her last visit. There was just an extra oversized lounge chair under the window, that had to be for Alfred. She noticed there was a small rag doll laying on the table and thought Rose must have been stitching it up for one of her friends or family she was working for.

Hazel entered the kitchen and started to make coffee. As the water was running from the sink, she faintly heard a small voice like a child say, "Hello." Hazel thought the childlike voice must be coming from the neighbors in the hall and did not stop the flow of water in the coffee pot. She heard the voice whisper again, "Hello," but this time it was closer and with the coffee pot still in her hand she turned around. Their eyes met first and Hazel blinked several times to focus. Out of the mouth of a little girl who mirrored the image of Hazel, the voice whispered again, "Hello!"

The smash of glass hitting the floor caused Rose and Alfred to swiftly arrive in the kitchen. Hazel was motionless, her hand still in the position of holding the handle of the coffee pot that was now shattered at her feet. Tears moved slowly down her cheeks and onto her neck causing a flood to build in the deep slope of her collar bone. Rose grabbed Abenia pulling her away from the glass. The room was silent except for the sound of running water from the kitchen faucet and Hazel's jubilant sobs. No words were spoken as Hazel took Abenia from Rose. She cradled Abenia in her arms holding so tight it felt like their hearts were beating in unison. Alfred turned off the water and he and Rose retreated back to the bedroom. Hazel quietly sat on the floor still holding and rocking her daughter. After five long years, they were together, and Hazel vowed this time no one or anything would ever separate them again.

Abenia was sleeping soundly in the bedroom that used to be Hazel's; the rag doll nestled underneath her arm. Hazel couldn't stop staring at her, afraid to look away thinking she might disappear, but she was real and here with her. She hadn't thought about what she was going to tell Daniel or his family. Maybe she could rewind her dream and they would just stay and build a life in Harlem. She was fearful of her old and new life colliding. As her mind wandered, she knew whatever her decision would be her daughter's well-being was now her priority.

Rose offered to take care of Abenia until Hazel had the opportunity to speak with Daniel. Rose felt a special connection with her young niece and welcomed this chance to bond. They agreed to initially tell people that Abenia was Hazel's sister. And that she needed to be taken care of until Hazel was able to disclose everything fully to Daniel and his family. Hazel was not comfortable misleading her husband but was more concerned with Abenia's happiness and how she would adjust to her new surroundings.

After a weekend in Harlem filled with moments of laughs, hugs and some tears, Hazel returned to Asbury Park with Abenia in tow. She decided to face this situation head-on with the truth and was ready to accept the refusal if that was to be. It was inevitable that the truth would be revealed at some point.

While at Rose's apartment, Hazel was brushing Abenia's hair and telling her how beautiful she was. She had dressed her in a vibrant red velvet dress with a big satin white bow that Rose made overnight. Abenia who believed Hazel was her sister, stated, "I wish you were my Mother." As Hazel pinned the small barrettes on the bottom of Abenia's curls she whispered in her ear, "Can you keep a secret?" Abenia nodded and Hazel said, "I am your Mother!" Abenia was so excited she began jumping and ran out into the living room and announced, "She's my Mother!" Hazel couldn't expect a child to keep a secret and did not want to put Abenia in that predicament. There had already been enough lies and deceit surrounding her conception and the first five years of her life. It all had to end now.

It was Sunday back in Asbury Park and the family was gathered at the table eating dinner when Hazel and Abenia arrived. Maggie looked surprised and before she could speak Morton dropped his fork on the floor as he was about to put it into his mouth. The clatter startled Abenia and she clutched her hands and arms around Hazel's waist. She seemed to be exceptionally skittish with unexpected sounds, perhaps there was a prior incident or trauma causing this reaction. Daniel let out a nervous chuckle and stood up to greet Hazel. He did not say anything but smiled kindly at Abenia.

Hazel had rehearsed what she wanted to say several times on the train ride home, but now she couldn't remember one word or thought. She knew if things didn't go well, she could stay with Marie and continue to work until she was able to secure employment in Harlem. Still standing with Abenia holding on, Hazel said, "This is my daughter. Her name is Abenia. I thought she was dead all these years which is why I did not tell you about her." Hazel stood still in silence gazing at the food on the dining room table beautifully displayed in the floral china platters Maggie was given by one of the families she worked for. Daniel had sat down by now and Morton was staring at him awaiting his response. After a few minutes, Daniel stood back up and said loudly, "Welcome home Abenia."

~

CHAPTER 7
FAMILY

Life for Hazel progressed as a wife to Daniel and mother to Abenia in Asbury Park. She continued to work as a domestic in various homes on the East Side of the city. Abenia was growing up and like Hazel had a fair complexion, auburn hair that waved as it met her shoulders and soft facial features. She attended the local Catholic school where she was often treated rudely by some of the nuns and other students. There were only a few students of color in the school and it was evident they were not welcome. The Walker family were active and devoted parishioners of St. Peter Claver Church which afforded Abenia this opportunity to attend the school at reduced tuition. Hazel was able to make the school payments in installments and also contribute to the building home loan Maggie and Morton held on the house they all resided in.

Although Hazel was not pleased with the school's environment or staff, she thought the education was stellar and wanted Abenia to have the best. Abenia proved to be a gifted opera singer and was a member of the school choir. She auditioned for a lead singing part in the school holiday show, but she was quickly passed over for that role and told her performance was needed in the group chorus. The lead roles were only given to the white students in the school. Incidents such as these were frequent at Mount Saint Clare and after years without any significant change, Hazel allowed Abenia to leave. She was enrolled in the public-school system that was more racially diverse.

After eleven years of marriage, Hazel and Daniel were finally expecting their first child. Maggie was overjoyed with the prospect of having a grandchild. Her constant nagging about when they were going to have a baby was all they heard. Hazel was delighted to be pregnant and hoped the new baby would inspire Daniel to find a better job that would ultimately enable them to move out of his parent's house.

It was a hopeful new year beginning with the birth of Margaret Rose in January. The healthy baby girl was named after her grandmother, Maggie, and great-aunt, Rose.

Fortunately, within a year after their daughter arrived, the house next door to Maggie and Morton became available to rent. It was a small bungalow painted green with white trim around the windows. The front and back porch was large with enough room for rocking chairs and a glider. There were two standard size bedrooms, a tiny bathroom, a living and dining room located in the center of the house, and a large kitchen with a pantry that led to a full basement. Most of the rooms were covered with floral wallpaper to accent the arched woodwork.

The house was owned by Morton's sister, Fannie, and her husband, Lawrence; therefore, the rent was reasonable. Hazel thought it was a great starter home for her family especially since Abenia was older and engaged to be married. She would be moving out and joining her future husband, Sonny, who was in the military and currently stationed overseas for two years. Hazel was initially reluctant about her daughter leaving home and getting married. However, she knew Abenia had a good head on her shoulders. She had grown into a lovely woman and was a pleasure to raise. Her willingness to work hard in school, assist around the house and never complain was reflective of her kind and generous demeanor. Truthfully, Hazel's hesitation was mostly based on her own feelings. She never wanted to be separated from Abenia after they were reunited years earlier.

The family settled into 204 with the new baby. Hazel felt elated to have a place that was their own. It was nice to have a kitchen where she could create the meals she selected. Living with Daniel's family all those years had been tough at times. Although she was embraced, they made it clear, especially Morton, that the arrangement was supposed to be temporary. However, Daniel showed no urgency to vacate his parent's home and Hazel was sure if Margaret wasn't born, they would still be all under the same roof.

Daniel was spending his days on Springwood Avenue handling the bookkeeping for the numbers racket and nights doing janitorial work for a company called, 'Klean Wipe' cleaning schools. Neither paid enough to cover the household expenses so Hazel kept working domestic jobs. Sometimes Hazel was able to bring Margaret with her to work, especially to the homes of families with children. While Maggie was ecstatic about having a grandchild, she rarely offered to assist with Margaret's care and when asked she was quick to decline and say she had to work. Fortunately, Hazel's dear friend Marie was always happy and willing to take care of Margaret.

Abenia and Margaret were her goddaughters and she adored them. Marie was also an amateur photographer always capturing photos of Margaret, everything from her first steps to her first day at school. Margaret was a gorgeous child with coffee brown skin, almond-shaped eyes, dark large ringlet curls, and Daniel's nose. She was curious, smart, personable, and enamored by all. Abenia cared for Margaret as if she were her own. The vast age difference between them inspired more coddling than sibling rivalry.

Rose relocated to Arlington, Virginia permanently with her husband Alfred and rekindled relationships with relatives in nearby Maryland. Hazel along with Abenia and Margaret, was able to visit Rose in Virginia for a long weekend. They also traveled to Maryland and Hazel finally had the opportunity to connect with her siblings; Elizabeth, Audrey, Lottie, Clarence, George, Robert, Andrew, William, James, and Lottie.

She was especially elated when she saw her sister Elizabeth, known as Reese. They were little girls the first time they met on the farm in Lancaster. Hazel never forgot holding Reese's hand under the tree and not being permitted to go home with her. Hazel was the big sister from up north and received a warm welcome from Reese and her other siblings.

Her mother, Julia, now a widow lived with one of Hazel's brothers in a nearby senior housing complex. Hazel learned her siblings did not have much growing up and some would consider them impoverished. It was hard times for Julia raising her children in what was called "Pigtown" with little means of support. She relied heavily on her daughter, Reese, to contribute financially and help provide for the family. Reese was more like a second mother to her younger siblings, except Lottie who was raised by other relatives in another area of Maryland. As adults, several siblings raised their families alongside each other in connected row houses in the city of Baltimore.

Over the years Hazel and all her siblings remained close. She frequently visited them in Maryland during the summer when the church ran their bus trips. Her brother, Clarence, called Snooks, also traveled to Asbury Park at least twice a year to deliver Hazel's favorite bushel of crabs and a pound of sugar.

The long weekend for Hazel turned into a week. She considered remaining in Arlington, Virginia with her girls Abenia and Margaret and not return to Asbury Park. Hazel was frustrated with everything at 204 including her marriage. Unbeknownst to Hazel or Daniel, the house was infested with roaches before they moved in. Enormous amounts of boric acid and pesticides placed around the baseboards to exterminate them fully were ineffective. Hazel did her best to maintain a clean home. They were also struggling to pay Uncle Lawrence the rent and keep the oil tank filled for heat.

An increased amount of Daniel's childhood friends were seeking and retaining employment at Fort Monmouth, the military base in Eatontown, a town north of Asbury Park. Everyone agreed Daniel would be a good candidate for an office position with his math skills. Although Daniel didn't drive and never obtained a driver's license, he had a lot of friends that he could travel with. Yet, again he declined any recommendations to join his friends, leaving Hazel disheartened.

It was a cloudy morning in Virginia approaching the second week with Rose and Alfred. Hazel had made up her mind to stay in Virginia. That night Hazel realized she had missed her period another month and could be pregnant. She knew having another child would alter her decision and she would need to return to Asbury Park.

Alexander arrived on time after an uneventful pregnancy, a healthy nine-pound baby boy with gobs of dark hair crowning his head, olive skin and ample lips like his father. Hazel immersed herself into motherhood; cloth diapers, glass bottles, washing, cleaning, and cooking. She also returned to her job as a domestic a few days a week. Money was desperately needed, making it necessary for her to work.

Margaret and Alexander were her inspiration. She wanted to give her children a childhood she did not have and that meant keeping the family together. Daniel was working part-time three to four nights a week with the janitorial service. Hazel had given up on him ever actually improving his employment status with a more stable and better paying job. She relied on the strength of her faith that the family's needs would be provided. Hazel was an active member at St. Peter Claver Church. She took the children to mass every Sunday and sat with her friend Marie and her in-laws. Hazel felt at peace in the church; It was her refuge.

The baby was called Alex to honor her grandfather. Deep down Hazel wanted to believe Papa Alec had loved her and his actions were based on his inability to stand up to Lina. She tried to remember the good times with him on the farm before Lina came into their lives and thankfully there were many good times to recall. Nevertheless, she would never return to Lancaster, although it was still her birthplace and first home. Hazel knew in order to be a loving mother she needed to let go of the resentment she held against Papa Alec and forgive him and only him. She could never and would never forget or forgive the abuse she endured from Lina and her family. It just wasn't in her heart to be remissive with them and she prayed God would empathize.

Several days of excessive sleeping propelled Hazel to take Alex to see the doctor. She didn't think it was normal for him to be sleeping so much and not waking up when he was hungry or when he needed to have his diaper changed. She had to force Alex to wake up to be fed. He was so different from Margaret who seldom wanted to sleep and was frequently fretful. Dr. Vincent's office was in walking distance like every place in town. Hazel left Margaret with Daniel and hoped to be back soon. She walked swiftly across town pushing the green checkered stroller with large spoked wheels. Her feet began to hurt as they arrived. It was a large white Victorian house with an expansive wrap around porch that gave access to a front and back door. They entered the second door towards the back of the porch which was for the doctor's patients.

The room was filled with people both black and white. Chairs lined one side of the office which looked like it used to be a living room and the other side sat a slightly worn sofa. Alex slept in the carriage as they waited to be seen and Hazel was anxious in anticipation of what the doctor might reveal about the baby's health. She paid the receptionist ten dollars which was the standard fee for the office visit.

After an hour they were escorted into a room that included a narrow hospital bed and two high back chairs. Dr. Vincent entered the room and asked Hazel to put Alex on the hospital bed. He woke up and began to cry when the doctor placed the bottom round portion of the stethoscope on his chest. The doctor asked questions about Alex's sleep pattern. He even suggested Hazel be happy that Alex sleeps and how most mothers complained that their babies didn't sleep enough. Hazel answered the doctor's questions and insisted something was wrong. She mentioned how Alex looked pale all the time and was lethargic. Dr. Vincent was familiar with the symptoms of Sickle Cell Anemia, he studied the disease in medical school. After the examination, he noticed how jaundiced Alex appeared, and was sure the baby was affected by the disease and in need of immediate treatment at the hospital.

The hospital was not a positive place for Hazel. She had been there two years prior and had to stay a few days after suffering a miscarriage. Now, she was here with her baby boy who was near death and in need of a blood transfusion. The doctors assured Hazel Alex's condition would improve after the treatment; however, he would also have long term medical issues for the rest of his life due to the disease. She was instructed on future care for Alex to help maintain adequate levels of iron and ways to minimize the pain during a sickle cell crisis.

Hazel couldn't fathom how she was going to manage it all and keep her sanity. She was already overwhelmed and not getting much help with the children. A sickly baby would add emotional and financial strain on the family. Hazel knew she had to stop working and prayed Daniel would be able to keep a roof over their heads.

Alex's health improved and he began to thrive. He was an unusually small child, but what he lacked in physical size he gained in mental ability. Margaret, equally as bright, was envious of the attention her little brother was getting because of his illness and would often tease him. It was a short-lived rivalry and one that Hazel would not tolerate. Especially, after Margaret took a pair of scissors and cut a chunk of Alex's hair; leaving him with a bald spot gleaming from the middle of his head. Hazel insisted they get along and Margaret complied embracing her role as the protective sister. Hazel was also expecting another baby and had to ensure the siblings respected each other. This was not a planned pregnancy, but the baby was going to be loved just the same.

Seven months later Hazel was back at the hospital. She

labored for over twenty hours before the doctors decided to perform an emergency cesarean section to deliver the baby. However, it was too late. The umbilical cord was wrapped around the baby's neck and with each push, the cord tightened causing her daughter to suffocate. Patricia was stillborn on St. Patrick's Day.

Although weakened with grief Hazel had to resume taking care of her family, there was no time to mourn. Once again, she found solace in the church, the rituals and reading of the scripture daily. Hazel was familiar with this type of ache, the longing to hold your child, and knowing it will never happen. It was difficult now to hug and kiss Margaret and Alex; thus, began Hazel's reluctance to show outward affection. She loved her children immensely and would do anything for them, but the ability to express her feelings with warm intimate gestures had diminished. Hazel was merely hanging on by a thread, not fully letting go of her emotions, afraid she wouldn't be able to withstand the enormity and be incapable of returning to herself. She suppressed her feelings, like she learned how to do as a child, and continued the tasks of wife and mother.

A year after losing Patricia, Hazel was expecting again. This time she was extremely anxious throughout the pregnancy. She couldn't seem to stay calm and felt she was going to jump out of her skin most of the time. During the seventh month of pregnancy, she noticed small droplets of blood in the toilet after using the bathroom. The doctor was concerned about the baby and ordered complete bed rest until the scheduled cesarean section delivery. Hazel was confined to a hospital bed for close to thirty days, which exaggerated her unsettledness. The possibility of losing another child forced her to pray harder and remain in bed for as long as she needed.

On a cold February morning, Phyllis Theresa entered the world early without the struggle of traveling down the birth canal. Consequently, she already had a preview of tension and worry while in the womb. Hazel hoped her beautiful, tiny, bald, wide-eyed baby girl wouldn't be scarred by her uneasiness during the pregnancy. She was eager to get home but sad about leaving Phyllis in the hospital. It was necessary as a premature birth to be monitored and not released until her weight was sufficient. She also missed Margaret and Alex and couldn't wait to sleep in her own bed. Abenia, now married, lived in a nearby town and in her absence helped Daniel and Maggie with the children; she was also expecting.

Hazel looked forward to Abenia and her husband starting a

family. They lived in a tiny cozy house that needed lots of TLC and fortunately Sonny was handy. He also wasn't afraid of work and soon after obtaining an honorable discharge from the military he joined a major construction company. Abenia adjusted well to married life but initially needed extra assistance from Hazel in the kitchen after some prepared burnt meals happened. Hazel was happy to share her cooking skills with her daughter.

Summer arrived quickly with a burst of heat that stifled the air. Early mornings were spent sitting on the porch with the children after preparing and feeding everyone breakfast. Phyllis, the baby slept in the carriage while Margaret and Alex played quietly in the wooden framed playpen. They soon fell off to sleep after a few tugs with the stuffed animals. It was the best time of the day for Hazel. As the children slept, she would first read verses in the Bible and then chapters in a book she borrowed from her friend Marie. They both shared the joy and escape reading provided. The genres varied, but both were partial to mysteries and historical non-fiction. Marie made it a point to weekly visit the majestic Asbury Park Library on Grand Avenue on her way home from work to take out books.

Hazel had no time to visit the library. It was difficult for her to leave the house with the children and she felt self-conscious about her attire. Frayed house dresses and stained aprons became her daily wardrobe. All the money earned was spent on the children and bills leaving none left for Hazel to buy clothes for herself. She didn't mind sacrificing for her children and was grateful to be home with them.

The following December Hazel's last baby, William Robert was born. He was also a cesarean delivery which extended their stay in the hospital. However, this time was different. William was a full-term birth without any medical concerns. He had mocha brown skin and thick dark hair. His head was shaped more oval than round like her other children, but he was healthy and smiled so angelic as he slept.

The two-bedroom household at 204 was overflowing with four children and two adults now. Hazel did her best to make the rooms livable. They squeezed two small beds and a crib in one room. The baby's bassinet fit in a corner of the other room along with a full-size bed and two tall dressers that were wedding gifts. The children loved playing in the side yard which had a massive oak tree that separated their house and Daniel's parents.

Alex continued to have his sickle cell crises, especially when he spent too much time playing with his siblings and friends. He would roll up on his knees and rock back and forth when the pain was unbearable. It became common to find him in this position in the bedroom while the other kids were outside. However, Hazel encouraged Alex to participate in activities when he could. She was frustrated and saddened that there was minimum relief for his condition. The doctors weren't certain how to treat him to prevent episodes. Over time he became resilient and learned to live with his discomfort. Alex did not want anyone to feel sorry for him and loathed being treated differently.

Phyllis and Alex had a close bond and were inseparable. She would stand in the doorway watching as he rocked himself to sleep often with tears in her eyes. Phyllis did not understand why her big brother had to hurt and why she could not fix him. As the middle child, she seemed to be able to fix everything; puzzles, broken toys, and sibling disagreements. Phyllis didn't mind getting dirty making mud pies with her brothers and climbing the oak tree in the side yard. She seemed tough but would cry quickly when frightened or nervous.

Hazel knew Phyllis' skittishness was probably a residual effect of what she felt when she was growing inside her womb. She would offer Phyllis praise to try and overcompensate for those feelings. William also looked up to his older brother and would follow him around the house and yard with a bottle still hanging from his mouth. Alex, Phyllis, and William were considered the three musketeers. It warmed Hazel's heart that her children were together and loved each other. They were experiencing the young sibling relationship she spent years dreaming about.

Hazel made sure the children attended Mass every Sunday. Alex and William were altar boys in the church while Margaret and Phyllis assisted the nuns in the rectory. To make sure they looked presentable Hazel washed their clothes by hand using the washboard in the basement and hung them on the clothesline that connected the back porches of 204 and Uncle Lawrence's house on Dewitt Avenue.

Hazel had a systematic way to hang the laundry. The clothespins were evenly placed on each item to ensure they did not wrinkle or tear the garment. She held a clothespin in her mouth after it was retrieved from her apron pocket. She then anchored the clothing item with both hands while attaching a pin on each side. This sequence was repeated over and over, along with Hazel humming a tune until the clothesline was filled.

Hazel enjoyed doing the laundry and savored the fresh smell of the clothes when they were dried from the warmth of the sun.

HAZEL AND DANIEL

~

CHAPTER 8
LIFE

Hazel returned to work part-time as a domestic while the children attended the neighborhood school during the day. She was employed by the Vaisman family as the maid and cook. Ian Vaisman was a prominent Dentist in Asbury Park. He and his wife, Millicent, had four children and two were the same age as Hazel's. Millicent Vaisman hosted her weekly bridge parties with her socialite girlfriends and many family gatherings. Their home on the East Side of the town was huge with the picturesque Deal Lake as the rear view. The Vaisman family were known around town to be nice people. Marie worked for one of the Vaisman's relatives and recommended Hazel to them when they needed additional help for an event.

The Vaisman's really liked Hazel and immediately offered her a full-time position. They paid Hazel cash every Friday and would also give a little extra at Christmas time. Mrs. Vaisman told Hazel the additional money was to help buy the children presents. Mr. or Mrs. Vaisman always offer to ride Hazel home when it got late. Hazel appreciated the ride; she was exhausted by the end of the day and walking was her means of transportation. In Asbury Park, there wasn't any bus service from one side of town to the other. Hazel accepted the opportunity to conserve her energy. Especially, knowing that when she got home her own family expected another full course meal. Hazel remained employed with the senior Vaisman family for many years. After Ian Vaisman passed away, she began the same duties for Stewart the eldest son, his wife, Marna, and their two boys in a neighboring town.

Church remained Hazel's haven especially on Sunday's. She took pride in reading the gospel as an auditor during mass. Most Saturday mornings when she didn't have to work, Hazel and other congregants who were friends assisted with volunteer activities for the parish including the operation of the church thrift shop. The church members also worked the yearly 'Shad Dinner' fundraiser. Daniel spent the day in the Catholic hall kitchen frying the delectable fish. The church ladies including

Maggie and Hazel prepared the sides of potato salad, collard greens, string beans, sweet potatoes, and cornbread. All the dinners were neatly packed and wrapped in aluminum foil with a knife and fork folded inside of a napkin. One slice of pound cake or sweet potato pie was also included with your dinner and topped off with one of the elders famous long brewed iced tea. These fun events were patronized by the church members and local community residents.

It was common for the people residing on the West Side to support each other and lend a helping hand. This was a close-knit area of the town, mostly black folks who attended church on Sunday mornings. Residents also gathered at the West Side Community Center for events. They participated and cheered in parades that showcased student drill teams as they strolled down the city's main street known as Springwood Avenue. It was a neighborly vibrate place to live and raise a family.

Unfortunately, like other small towns, there was the lure of deviance for the youth to find, even without looking. Hazel's children were not protected from the perils of drug abuse, teen pregnancy, incarceration, and mental illness.

Although, she did her best to keep them away from harm and heartache both came knocking on the door at 204.

Alex, small in size was brilliant, overwhelmingly kind, hand-some and gifted with a voice similar to Eddie Kendrick from the Temptations. He never griped when he was sick and debilitated with pain. Everyone liked Alex and laughed at his humor. He could make Hazel smile on her worst day with a funny gesture. Alex was not fond of attending school regularly, but he still excelled academically. He preferred surrounding himself with music and enjoyed singing. Along with some friends, he assembled a singing group of local guys. They practiced vocals and dance routines in the basement most weekends and dreamed of becoming famous enough to appear on the Ed Sullivan Show.

Sadly, Alex started hanging out with the wrong crowd, smoking cigarettes and eventually turned to drugs; mostly heroine, initially to ease his body aches and pain, but eventually, the drug use became a habit. Despite his illness and the limitations associated with Sickle Cell Disease, Alex began an early life of committing crimes to support his habit. This behavior grew in intensity as he aged, which precipitated his incarceration more times than Hazel wanted to remember.

It was hard for Hazel to accept Alex's inability to stay out of prison. She spent many hours praying he would not die behind bars. While incarcerated Alex utilized his excellent writing skills to assist other inmates and would often review their legal documents to provide clarity. He wrote Hazel lovely letters expressing his remorse and sorrow for his actions. Hazel did not give up on her son and was certain his life would have turned out differently if he had not been exposed to drugs. Regretfully, the majority of Alex's life was spent with restrictions and Hazel believed he was now incapable of functioning fully in the real world without them. Thus, leaving him with limited ability to be a father to his child.

Margaret had grown into a beauty with wit and intelligence that matched any ivy league scholars. She did well in school, had lots of friends and was considered popular. Hazel admired her confidence and independence. Margaret also sang like a Supreme and was a featured singer at the yearly Easter Monday Ball held on the Asbury Park boardwalk. Her vocal talents were recognized early by the local piano teacher during a recital. She later became the lead singer in a group called the Creatives, but soon developed a love of dancing. Margaret's skill of dance was evident when she won the 'Mashed Potato Dance Contest' at the West Side Community Center.

Dance halls were forming in Asbury Park and the surrounding towns and she didn't miss an opportunity to attend. Margaret and her girlfriends spent hours dressing, putting on makeup, teasing their hair, and practicing their dance moves in the bedroom mirror. They would sneak a cigarette smoke in the bathroom before rushing off to a dance. Hazel enjoyed the lively banter from the girls in the house and would often cook their favorite foods. They all viewed Hazel like a second mom.

At one of the dances, as she entered the school gym, Margaret noticed the tall handsome guy leaning against the side of the bleachers and holding a basketball. He had a strong chin, thick black curly hair, caramel skin, and soft dark eyes. Margaret had never seen such a striking face before and was immediately smitten. He seemed to perk up when he noticed her too. It was a special holiday dance in a nearby town and Margaret along with her girlfriends stood out from the crowd. They were gorgeous girls with bouffant hair and pencil skirts ready to light up the dance floor.

Margaret and the basketball guy stared at each other most of the night. Even when she was dancing, she would catch him glimpsing at her. He mustered up the nerve to ask her to dance right before the last song was played. It was a slower pace song and he seemed to stumble trying to keep the beat. Margaret took his hands and he followed her lead. When the song ended, he smiled and thanked her for not laughing at his clumsiness. She just smiled back. She didn't realize they were still holding hands when he asked what her name was and for a minute she couldn't remember. She blurted, "Margaret, but my friends call me Peggy." The handsome basketball guy said, "My friends call me Gary."

After months of attending dances with Gary and a one-time intimate encounter, Margaret became pregnant. They were both teens still in high school and clueless about their future as a couple or parenthood. Gary's mother thought they should get married, but Hazel was against it. She knew Margaret wasn't ready to be a wife or a mother for that matter. During the pregnancy, Margaret and Gary became distant, largely because Hazel was angry and limited their interactions.

During Margaret's last trimester Hazel attempted to place her in a home for unwed mothers with the agreement the baby would be put up for adoption after delivery. She traveled via train to meet with the nuns who ran the home and was told a nominal monthly fee would be required to house Margaret until the delivery of the baby.

Hazel and Daniel were already struggling to make ends meet and could not afford another expense; therefore, she returned home and told Margaret they would be keeping the baby.

Hazel was not happy the family would have another mouth to feed, but she loved her daughter and wanted to support her. Hazel agreed to take care of the baby while Margaret returned to high school to continue her studies and complete secretarial courses. Margaret was already guaranteed a good job at the local telephone company and would start after she graduated. Margaret, on a blustery winter morning, before the sun peeked through, gave birth to a baby girl, named Kelly Lynn.

Phyllis, a pretty girl with large bright eyes, looked most like Hazel out of the children she had with Daniel. They shared the small space between their front teeth, shapely legs, and athletic arms. As the middle child, Phyllis was eager to please others and stood out in academics and charm. She often seemed nervous shaking her leg while sitting or picking her nails when no one looked. However, none of Phyllis' outward agitations over-shadowed her drive and strong determination to succeed.

Hazel was very proud of her preemie girl and admired her ability to overcome in utero chaos and become the first in the family to attend college. Phyllis was the captain of the high school cheerleading squad, member of the drama and debate clubs, plus she was best friends with the local doctor's daughter.

She left 204 for college and did not return to Asbury Park after graduating.

Hazel lived vicariously through her overachieving daughter as she traveled the world spending a year abroad in Spain on a student exchange program. The student exchange program required an enrollment fee of $1,000 which Hazel and Daniel did not have in full by the required due date.

Hazel was able to borrow the money from The Vaisman family and never missed a weekly payment until they were paid in full. Graduate school for Phyllis was completed in Washington, DC where she stayed.

William, nicknamed Billy was a cute little boy. He grew to be tall and lanky like his grandfather, Morton. Billy had thick curly brown hair and his eyelashes had grown so long they touched the tip of his eyebrows. He adored his older siblings and would always follow them around the house. Billy had a tough time doing his schoolwork and keeping up with the class. The teachers complained he didn't pay attention and needed to try harder. Hazel was frustrated with the school's attempts to educate Billy and had to intercede many times on his behalf. Billy eventually became disillusioned with school and it was a challenge to get him out of bed in the morning. However, he spent hours drawing sketches, watching movies, listening to music, and browsing comic books. It was difficult to get Billy to read, unlike his siblings who absorbed every piece of literature they got their hands on. But amazingly Billy taught himself how to play chess and he became an exceptional player.

News spread of his talents and people all around town came to 204 to challenge him to a chess match. Hazel was proud of Billy's proficiency to master the game of chess and win his matches against opponents. Indeed, she was disappointed with his difficulties in school, but she indulged his creative endeavors. Hazel knew Billy was intelligent, yet believed he was promoted yearly without ensuring he was learning. Nonetheless, Billy adapted and was able to graduate from high school.

The riots of Asbury Park occurred the Summer of 1970. Billy was a recent graduate from high school. Groups of young people his age and other residents were actively encouraging the administration at the high school to diversify the curriculum and include content pertaining to people of color. They were also seeking to increase the availability of employment opportunities at the beachfront establishments for the youth of color in the city. Students and community members organized a peaceful protest.

The walk started at the beginning of Springwood Avenue on the West Side and was supposed to end after crossing over the railroad tracks onto the East Side of the street. However, the crowds grew quickly, and people opposed to the walk filtered into the streets. Pushing and shoving ensued and tempers flared. No one knows for sure how the first fire started. But it continued spreading down each block, burning the shops and businesses that had served the community for years. Some people started going into the local shops and businesses demanding goods, busting windows, and breaking doors. The town was under siege and the National Guard was called in to calm and control the city.

Billy was one of the peaceful protestors and as he walked with the crowd he was shot. Hazel was summoned by a neighbor to get down to Springwood Avenue because Billy had been hurt during the protest. Hazel ran out the back door cutting through Dewitt Avenue with Kelly right behind her. They arrived at the corner of Dewitt and Springwood Avenues and were immediately stopped by the National Guard troops. All you could hear were loud sirens and yells for individuals to back up. Smoked filled the air like a fog and people were erratically moving on the sidewalk and into the street with items that had been looted from the shops. It was a chaotic scene as Hazel stood there on the street corner holding Kelly's hand. She was fearful and expecting the worse regarding Billy.

Hazel was instructed that all injured people were taken to the local hospital. She quickly walked back to the house with Kelly and called a taxi to drive her to the emergency room of the area hospital. When she arrived at the emergency room it was filled with parents like herself waiting to hear about their children. Several hours later the doctor came into the waiting area and started calling out names. When he shouted William, Hazel jumped up and rushed over to the doctor. The doctor assured Hazel; Billy would be okay. He had been shot in the groin and lost a lot of blood, but the bullet had been successfully removed. Hazel later learned that warning shots were expelled to disperse the crowd on Springwood Avenue and somehow Billy was injured.

It was sudden when Billy started to hear voices and exhibit signs of paranoia. He began smoking packs of cigarettes and marijuana daily. He said weed quieted the voices in his head and helped him sleep. Billy only left the house to get his smoking essentials. He isolated himself from family and friends. After an episode where he pushed Daniel, his father, through the glass front door Billy was admitted to a psychiatric hospital for observation and treatment.

Billy was diagnosed with schizophrenia and prescribed medication. He hated taking the medication because it made him feel lethargic and caused excessive weight gain.

Drinking 40-ounce beers became a substitution for the medication, which only enhanced his paranoia. Hazel thought she was helping her last child by providing him with money when he insisted. However, she could not protect him from contracting pneumonia and eventually dying from a heart attack before he turned thirty-three. Losing another child was indescribable for Hazel. Although, Billy was grown; he was still her baby. She also knew he suffered for many years and prayed he was finally at peace.

Hazel's firstborn Abenia was now an established wife and mother. Her family moved from the tiny house to a nearby suburb of beautiful homes with rolling lawns and large cement driveways that led up to double garages. They were one of the first black families to purchase a home in a new development located near the hospital that served the local towns. Abenia for many years was a stay at home mother and was active in numerous social clubs. When she started working outside the home, she spared no expense in showering Hazel with unique garments, jewelry, and household items. She wanted her mother to have the best and knew that she deserved it. Hazel felt like a glamorous movie star wearing her daughter's gifts to mass on Sundays.

Abenia was generous, kind, and loving not only with Hazel but also with other family members and friends. She and her husband, Sonny, opened their home to family whenever they needed a place to stay, a car to borrow, or financial assistance in an emergency. Family gatherings were frequent at their home in the Gables where laughter and love were abundant. Abenia, like her mother Hazel, was the epitome of beauty and grace. Hazel admired her first child and was grateful she had a good life.

~

CHAPTER 9
TIME

Over the years Hazel kept her promise to be a caring mother. She managed to create a nurturing home despite the adversities and disappointments she encountered while raising her children. She always put the children's needs first, listened intently to their concerns, offered her words of wisdom, and loved them unconditionally. When times were tough Hazel found the means to cook amazing meals accompanied with the right prayer that nourished their bodies and minds. Her marriage to Daniel remained dutiful without the overly open expression of adoration. However, she was grateful their union produced children and believed she survived Lancaster for this purpose.

Daniel turned down the offer to take over Skinny's pool hall on Springwood Avenue after Skinny's untimely passing. Instead, he began writing the numbers full time at 204. Hazel was not consulted prior to this arrangement and it became a household routine of strangers coming and going from early morning until mid-afternoon. It wasn't unusual for Hazel to wake up and find her dining room table surrounded with Daniel's clients either sitting or standing holding their cash in one hand and written slips of numbers in the other. Daniel's voice was blaring and could be heard repeating the three digits given to him by his clients as he wrote the numbers in his ledger.

The house, although meager, was no longer a home, but a vessel for excessive traffic and business transactions. During this time 204 was still occupied by Billy and Kelly, who had six years between them and were being raised as brother and sister. They had no sense of privacy; Kelly often felt anxious and frightened with the intrusiveness. Daniel thought that most of the people who dropped by were harmless. Most were primarily local residents, and some were from surrounding neighborhoods. They all had dreams of winning big enough to purchase homes, buy a new car, or pay off some bills. Daniel frequently added an extra ten cents on all the numbers he collected in hopes to acquire his own fortune. Unfortunately, that big win dream never materialized.

Many of the people who played the numbers regularly in

Asbury Park died owing Daniel money because he allowed everyone to run a tab and most never paid up. They vowed to catch up on payday, when they hit or when so and so paid them. These assurances seldom occurred. Hazel never understood why Daniel continued writing the numbers; when he received a minimum monetary benefit. Perhaps, it was Daniel's desire to avoid a structured day job or his inability to stop once Skinny died. The electric and oil bill was constantly delinquent. Hazel was thankful they were renting the house from Uncle Lawrence and they were allowed to pay the rent weekly. This type of arrangement made it easier to manage the payments.

Hazel loved children and started babysitting for an extra source of income. She didn't earn much money since she frequently allowed some of the parents to pay when they could. Hazel had a soft spot for helping others who were trying their best. She understood about folks having difficult times while working and raising families, as she did at 204. Hard times were common especially the winter mornings when everyone in the family had to get dressed in the kitchen or freeze. They took turns standing in front of the gas stove with the oven door open to warm up. There was no heat when the oil man refused to make a delivery until the bill was paid. Weekly grocery shopping consisted of a few bags of standard 'Ideal' products, however, Kool-Aid packets, bread, and Karo syrup were must-haves. They couldn't afford name brand items and ice cream was a monthly luxury. Hazel said, "Daniel thought he was going to get rich sitting in that chair writing those numbers." But the only thing he got was a little notoriety and eventually locked up.

It was summertime and people were enjoying the day sitting on their steps and porches. The children were riding bikes and windows were down on cars as they drove by. The traffic of clients continued at 204 and for some reason, it seemed to have increased with the warmer weather.

On this sunny day, Hazel was busy hanging clothes on the line in the backyard while keeping a watchful eye on her great-grandson, Korey, as he played in the grass. Kelly, like her mother Margaret, had given birth to a son at a young age. However, she managed to graduate high school early, work two jobs and attended college full-time. Once again, Hazel, obviously disappointed was still the anchor of love and support. She cared for Korey while Kelly attended a local college during the day and worked in retail at night. Hazel also continued working for the Vaisman's on Saturdays. She encouraged her granddaughter to continue her education and not settle for a life that was mediocre, especially since she now had a child to raise.

Daniel refused to take heed when told about the strange car in the neighborhood that sat on the corner for hours. The people inside the car were not familiar faces. They were seen using binoculars and jotting down notes throughout the day. Hazel was in the backyard when she heard the shouts coming from inside the house. She ran up the steps onto the porch but was unable to open the back-screen door. Someone inside was holding it shut as she pulled on the handle. She was able to see through the screen that police officers were standing in the kitchen and gathered in the dining room. One of the officers approached the screen and said that the house was being raided and she was not allowed inside.

Hazel couldn't see Daniel from where she stood but knew when she left the house, he was sitting in his chair at the head of the dining room table. He always sat there while conducting business. She was unexpectedly calm waiting on the back porch probably because she didn't want to appear upset in front of her great-grandson. Keeping him amused in the yard knowing her house was being ransacked was nerve-racking. Korey also needed to use the bathroom. Hazel knew he would be scared with all the commotion going on inside the house, so she walked him around the side of the garage and allowed him to pee on the ground. He laughed as he splattered the dirt and asked could he do that again.

A female police officer came outside onto the porch and told Hazel that Daniel was being arrested for illegal gambling and that he would be able to call her after he was processed at the police station. Hazel asked if she could see Daniel before he was taken away. She felt a knot in the pit of her stomach and held her hands tightly clenched in the pockets of her apron. Daniel was escorted to the door with his arms held behind his back. Hazel pressed her head gently against the screen and spoke softly to her husband almost in a whisper and said, "You're going to be alright." She sat on the back steps for a while watching Korey as he circled the yard with his arms stretched wide pretending to be an airplane and after a silent prayer and a few deep breaths she said out loud the five words she often recited to summon peace, "NOW IS THE ACCEPTABLE TIME!"

~

CHAPTER 10
CLOSURE

Much had changed for Hazel during the time Daniel spent in jail for his role in the illegal gambling operation in the city. She hesitantly left her home and joined Kelly with husband Stacy, son Korey, and daughter Kourtney when they purchased a house and settled in the northern part of the state. The church she grew to love was torn down due to severe building damage and lack of funding for repairs.

Sadly, over the years Asbury Park had become permeated with increased crime and minimum employment opportunities. The horrendous riots of the 70's stifled the West Side and people were either relocating out of the state or settling in other areas of New Jersey. Many of Hazel's family members and friends, including her dearest friend Marie, were no longer living. Emotionally, it was a time of dismay for Hazel; yet, she continued to remain committed to her faith and family.

Hazel learned at an early age to be resilient when all you have is the dream of something better. To love when all you felt was abandoned and betrayed. To be fearless when others around you lacked courage. To exhibit loyalty when it would be ingenious to walk away.

She reunited with Daniel Howard Lee when he was released after completing his sentence, both now in their late 70's. The marriage lasted for 67 years until his passing from congestive heart failure. Hazel wept as she sat in the hospital room with her husband for the last time. She tenderly placed her hand on his forehead and said, "See you on the other side."

The children, grandchildren and great-grandchildren were Hazel's motivation for living. She found solace in walking and would walk her great-granddaughter Kourtney to the bus stop every morning before school. While waiting on the corner they would play the game patty cake. Each slapping the other's hands over and under until Hazel finally won. They both laughed and Kourtney would giggle loudly causing people who passed by in cars on their way to work to stop and stare. Some smiled, while others seemed annoyed at their joy. Hazel didn't care who looked and would often say, "Misery loves company, some people just don't like to see others happy."

Hazel was always the confidante, playmate, and protector with her children, grandchildren, and all the children she took care of. Even as she aged, she demonstrated poise and confidence.

One morning after Kourtney boarded the school bus, as Hazel stepped off the sidewalk two large Doberman pinschers appeared. She recognized them as the neighbor's dogs and speculated they must have gotten loose. They circled around her growling and barking preventing her from moving. Hazel too proud to walk with a regular cane carried the handle of an old broom on her walks, just in case her knee might give out. She commenced whacking the sidewalk hard with that old broom handle over and over while standing firm until the dogs retreated. Hazel unshaken proceeded to cross the street and walked gingerly home.

Hazel sustained her love and passion for reading, although consequently, a stroke left her with only one eye with substantial vision. She enjoyed her daily scriptures along with the numerous books of various genres she received from Kelly; both were avid readers and would have in-depth discussions about the books they read.

In her late 80's Hazel had to have a pacemaker implanted

when her heart started to skip beats and slowed down. She seemed content in her golden years and her mind remained sharp. Hazel remembered everything about her life in Lancaster, Harlem and Asbury Park. She became more descriptive as she shared many of her experiences and stories when she traveled with Kelly in the car. Kelly treasured their time together on long rides, mainly after one of Hazel's doctor's appointments. Kelly listened intently and absorbed each word.

One chilly Sunday Hazel slept in, which was unusual. She maintained her routine of rising early, even if she had been up late reading. Kelly felt a sense of apprehension when she walked up to the steps to Hazel's bedroom. Somehow Kelly knew. The morning just seemed different. Kelly didn't want to think about what could be as she opened Hazel's door slightly. Kelly peeked in and Hazel was sleeping, snoring and motionless. Kelly opened the door wider and called, "GG" several times. She didn't respond.

Ten days of sleeping and still snoring allowed loved ones to gather. The hospital room was filled with flowers, laughter, hugs, and mostly tears. Hazel had accomplished her dream of having a family one that now expanded four generations. Her sacrifice and faithful spirit enabled the family to unselfishly release the earth's hold. It was the family's turn to put Hazel first.

On that early October morning, Kelly listened, like when one of Hazel's stories was being revealed. No car rides this time, just the sound of a still sky, brightly illuminated solely by the light of the moon when Hazel, Kelly's dear grandmother peacefully closed the book on her life at the age of 95.

GLOSSARY

Arlington National Cemetery: The United States military cemetery in Arlington County, Virginia, across the Potomac River from Washington, D.C., in whose 624 acres the dead of the nation's conflicts has been buried, beginning with the Civil War, as well as reinterred dead from earlier wars. The United States Department of the Army, a component of the United States Department of Defense (DoD), controls the cemetery.

Asbury Park, New Jersey: A city in Monmouth County, New Jersey, located on the Jersey Shore and part of the New York City Metropolitan Area. It was ranked the sixth-best beach in New Jersey in the 2008 Top 10 Beaches Contest sponsored by the New Jersey Marine Sciences Consortium.

Atwood, Margaret: Novelist, Poet (2019) Quote: "In the end, we'll all become stories."

Baltimore, Maryland: The third-most populous county located in the U.S. state of Maryland and is part of the Baltimore metropolitan area and Baltimore-Washington metropolitan area (a combined statistical area). Along with Washington,

D.C. and its suburbs, Baltimore County forms the southern anchor of the Northeast megalopolis, which stretches northward to Boston.

Belmar, New Jersey: A borough in Monmouth County, New Jersey, United States. The city acquired its current name, Borough of Belmar, on November 20, 1890. The borough's name means "beautiful sea" in Italian.

Bly, Nellie: American Journalist, (2019), Ten Days in a Mad House, (1887).

Cab Calloway: Cabell Calloway (December 25, 1907 – November 18, 1994) was an American jazz singer, dancer, and bandleader. He was associated with the Cotton Club in Harlem, New York City, where he was a regular performer. Calloway was a master of energetic scat singing and led one of the United States' most popular big bands from the start of the 1930s to the late 1940s. Calloway's band included trumpeters Dizzy Gillespie and Adolphus "Doc" Cheatham, saxophonists Ben Webster and Leon "Chu" Berry, New Orleans guitarist Danny Barker, and bassist Milt Hinton. Calloway continued to perform until his death in 1994 at the age of 86.

Cotton Club: The Cotton Club was a New York City

nightclub located in Harlem on 142nd Street and Lenox Avenue from 1923 to 1935, then briefly in the midtown Theater District from 1936 to 1940. The club operated most notably during the United States' era of Prohibition. The club was a whites-only establishment, but featured many of the most popular black entertainers of the era, including musicians Duke Ellington, Chick Webb, Louis Armstrong, Count Basie, Fats Waller, Willie Bryant; vocalists Adelaide Hall, Ethel Waters, Cab Calloway, Bessie Smith,, Avon Long, the Dandridge Sisters, the Will Vodery Choir, The Mills Brothers, Nina Mae McKinney, Billie Holiday, Lena Horne; and dancers Bill Robinson, The Nicholas Brothers, Charles 'Honi' Coles, Leonard Reed, Stepin Fetchit,The Four Step Brothers, Jeni Le Gon and Earl Snakehips Tucker.

Count Basie: William James "Count" Basie (August 21, 1904 – April 26, 1984) was an American jazz pianist, organist, bandleader, and composer. He was born in Red Bank, New Jersey. In 1935, Basie formed his own jazz orchestra, the Count Basie Orchestra, and in 1936 took them to Chicago for a long engagement and their first recording. He led the group for almost 50 years, creating innovations like the use of two "split" tenor saxophones, emphasizing the rhythm section, riffing with a big band, using arrangers to broaden their sound, and others.

Duke Ellington: Edward Kennedy "Duke" Ellington (April 29, 1899 – May 24, 1974) was an American composer, pianist, and leader of a jazz orchestra, which he led from 1923 until his death over a career spanning more than fifty years. Born in Washington, D.C., Ellington was based in New York City from the mid-1920s onward and gained a national profile through his orchestra's appearances at the Cotton Club in Harlem.

Eddie Kendricks: Edward James Kendrick (December 17, 1939 – October 5, 1992), best known by the stage name Eddie Kendricks, was an American singer and songwriter. Noted for his distinctive falsetto singing style, Kendricks co-founded the Motown singing group The Temptations and was one of their lead singers from 1960 until 1971. His was the lead voice on such famous songs as "The Way You Do The Things You Do", "Get Ready", and "Just My Imagination (Running Away with Me)". As a solo artist, Kendricks recorded several hits of his own during the 1970s, including the number-one single "Keep On Truckin'".

Ed Sullivan Show: The Ed Sullivan Show was an American

television variety show that ran on CBS from June 20, 1948, to June 6, 1971, and was hosted by New York entertainment columnist Ed Sullivan. In 2002, The Ed Sullivan Show was ranked #15 on TV Guide's 50 Greatest TV Shows of All Time. In 2013, the series finished No. 31 in TV Guide Magazine's 60 Best Series of All Time.

Four Step Brothers: The Four Step Brothers were an African American dance group. The group started out as a trio in 1925. Dubbed "The Eight Feet of Rhythm," the group soon traveled with Duke Ellington. The quartet was the first black act to perform at Radio City Music Hall, the first to appear at the Chez Paree Club in Chicago and the first to break television's color bar. The group became known for their complex dance routines. The "Brothers" incorporated snake hips, five-tap wings, slides, Afro-Cuban movements, rhythm (jazz) tap, the camel walk, the strut, and straight acrobatics.

Harlem, New York: Is a neighborhood in the northern section of the New York City borough of Manhattan. It is bounded roughly by Frederick Douglass Boulevard, St. Nicholas Avenue, and Morningside Park on the west; the Harlem River and 155th Street on the north; Fifth Avenue on the east; and

Central Park North on the south. Harlem's history has been defined by a series of economic boom-and-bust cycles, with significant population shifts accompanying each cycle. Harlem was predominantly occupied by Jewish and Italian Americans in the 19th century, but African American residents began to arrive in large numbers during the Great Migration in the 20th century. In the 1920s and 1930s, Central and West Harlem were the focus of the "Harlem Renaissance", an outpouring of artistic work without precedent in the American-black community.

Joe Louis: Joseph Louis Barrow (May 13, 1914 – April 12, 1981), best known as Joe Louis was an American professional boxer who competed from 1934 to 1951. He reigned as the world heavyweight champion from 1937 to 1949 and is considered to be one of the greatest heavyweight boxers of all time. Nicknamed the "Brown Bomber", Louis' championship reign lasted 140 consecutive months, during which he participated in 26 championship fights. The 27th fight, against Ezzard Charles in 1950, was a challenge for Charles' heavyweight title and so is not included in Louis' reign. He was victorious in 25 title defenses.

Lancaster County, Virginia: Lancaster County is a county located on the Northern Neck in the Commonwealth of Virginia. Located on the Northern Neck near the mouth of the Rappahannock River, Lancaster County is part of the Northern Neck George Washington Birthplace wine-growing region recognized by the United States as an American Viticultural Area. Lancaster County is the most densely populated county in the Northern Neck. The largest town in Lancaster County is Kilmarnock, Virginia.

Lena Horne: Lena Mary Calhoun Horne (June 30, 1917 – May 9, 2010) was an American singer, dancer, actress, and civil rights activist. Horne's career spanned over 70 years appearing in film, television, and theater. Horne joined the chorus of the Cotton Club at the age of 16 and became a nightclub performer before moving to Hollywood.

Savoy: The Savoy Ballroom was a large ballroom for music and public dancing located at 596 Lenox Avenue, between 140th and 141st Streets in the Harlem neighborhood of Manhattan, New York City Lenox Avenue was the main thoroughfare through upper Harlem. Poet Langston Hughes calls it the Heartbeat of Harlem in Juke Box Love Song, and he set his work "Lenox Avenue: Midnight" on the legendary street. The Savoy was one of many Harlem hot spots along Lenox, but it was the one to be called the "World's Finest Ballroom."

Sickle Cell Anemia Disease: A blood abnormality in the oxygen-carrying protein hemoglobin found in red blood cells. This leads to a rigid, sickle-like shape. Problems in sickle cell disease typically begin around 5 to 6 months of age. Health problems develop, such as attacks of pain ("sickle cell crisis"), anemia, swelling in the hands and feet, bacterial infections and stroke.

St. Peter Claver Church: A Roman Catholic Church, formally located on Springwood Avenue Asbury Park, NJ on the Westside of the city. The congregants were primarily African American and Hispanic.

Supremes: The Supremes were an American female singing group and the premier act of Motown Records during the 1960s. Founded as The Primettes in Detroit, Michigan, in 1959, the Supremes were the most commercially successful of Motown's acts and are, to date, America's most successful vocal group] with 12 number one singles on the Billboard Hot 100. By 1965, the Supremes were international stars. They toured the world, becoming almost as popular abroad as they were in the US.

Turf Lounge: Nightclub located in Asbury Park on the Westside of the city, frequented by African American singers and musicians.

Virginia: Officially the Commonwealth of Virginia, is a state in the Southeastern and Mid-Atlantic regions of the United States located between the Atlantic Coast and the Appalachian Mountains.

Wikipedia. Wikipedia.org, Accessed April 2019.

ACKNOWLEDGMENTS

I would like to first thank my husband and biggest supporter, my 'Roney' for listening to excerpts read over and over while he was trying to sleep. Your encouragement and ability to push me through when obstacles hindered my progression was paramount. You are Mr. Magic!

Special thank you to my son, Korey, and daughter, Kourtney who had the privilege to embrace GG. Thank you for supporting my dream of writing and cheering for me as I accomplished this bucket list achievement.

Lots of thanks to my grandson, KJ for your encouragement and our weekly pizza dates that allowed me to share our legacy.

Special gratitude to my mom, Peggy who recognized my vision. Thank you for giving me the courage to express myself genuinely. I write because you passed on your dream of writing.

Much appreciation to my aunts and uncles; Bena, Phyllis, Alex, and Billy for their unwavering affection and support over the years, which led to this point of reflection on facets of our shared history.

Thank you to my in-laws, Al and Adele for their constant prayers, encouragement, and Harlem memories.

Thank you, Chance, my furbaby who stayed by my side when I

wrote late at night keeping me alert with breaks to rub his belly.

What About My Friends ….

Thank you to my dear friends who either held my hand, sent cards of encouragement, listened to my ideas, offered words of support, shared a quote, baked my favorite goodies, gave me a hug, prayed for me, made me laugh, picked up my coffee, or just believed I could write and finish this book. You know who you are, and I appreciate all your support…

Much gratitude to Victor who sent daily texts of encouragement and kept me in his prayers at Mass. Elaine and my niece Ashley (Lady A) for always checking on my progress and offering words of support.

Special thank you to my NJ1 GOG Chapter Sister-Friends; Iris, Karen, Michele, Kelli, Bevereley. Your encouragement and support mean the world to me. I am looking forward to a special Chat & Chew at our favorite place, Nordy's Cafe. Extending extra appreciation to Dr. Karen for your editing and proofreading skills.

Thank you to the Sisterhood of Go On Girl! Book Club, Inc. for expanding my literary world with books that accentuate pride and for providing a vessel that introduced me to amazing authors.

Thank you to my high school English teacher, Ms. Mitchell for sharing her book selections with me and my grandmother, always seeing my potential and never placing judgment.

Thank you to the students in my Computer Class who teach me each day to never give up!

Shout-out to Asbury Park for the memories...

Blue Bishops!

Last, but not least, my grandmother, Hazel, who constantly said, "I need to write a book about my life." I would respond, "I'm going to write your book." Here it is GG!
I hope you are pleased. Thank you so much for entrusting me with your stories.

NOW IS THE ACCEPTABLE TIME

ABOUT THE AUTHOR

Kelly Walker Edwards was raised in a small town at the Jersey Shore. She is an avid reader, technology enthusiast, and summa cum laude graduate. Kelly is married, with two children, one grandson, and a rescued Yorkie Poo.